Thank you...

... for purchasing this copy of Reading for Literacy for ages 7-8. We hope that you find our worksheets, teachers' notes and display materials helpful as part of your programme of literacy activities.

Please note that photocopies can only be made for use by the purchasing institution. Supplying copies to other schools, institutions or individuals breaches the copyright licence. Thank you for your help in this.

This Reading for Literacy book is part of our growing range of educational titles. Most of our books are individual workbooks but, due to popular demand, we are now introducing a greater number of photocopiable titles especially for teachers. You may like to look out for:

READING FOR LITERACY for Reception
and for ages 5-7, 7-8, 8-9, 9-10, 10-11

WRITING FOR LITERACY for ages 5-7, 7-8, 8-9, 9-10, 10-11

SPELLING FOR LITERACY for ages 5-7, 7-8, 8-9, 9-10, 10-11

NUMERACY TODAY for ages 5-7, 7-9, 9-11

HOMEWORK TODAY for ages 7-8, 8-9, 9-10, 10-11

BEST HANDWRITING for ages 7-11

To find details of our other publications, please visit our website: **www.acblack.com**

Andrew Brodie Publications

ABOUT THIS BOOK

As with all our photocopiable resource books we have kept the teachers' notes to a minimum as we are well aware that teachers will use their own professionalism in using our materials.

At the start of each Unit we list some of the National Literacy Strategy Objectives that the Unit may cover. We are grateful to the Department for Education and Skills for their permission to quote the Objectives.

Some of the Units are linked to others as indicated by their titles.

Many Units feature reading activities that can be undertaken individually or in a small group situation, alongside the teacher or support assistant.

Some Units could be copied on to Overhead Projector Transparencies for use with a large group or the whole class.

The Units vary in their level of difficulty and teachers will match Units to the ability levels of the pupils in their classes.

Most Units are four pages long. All of them provide worthwhile activities as well as useful practice for tests.

Extracts from the National Literacy Strategy Framework for Teaching, © Crown copyright 1998, reproduced by kind permission of the Department for Education and Skills.

Contents ...
Year 3

Contents ...

Year 3

Contents ...
Year 3

Term 3

The objective indicated on the contents pages, is the main focus for each Unit. Each Unit can, however, be used for many different objectives and further suggestions of objectives are found at the start of each Unit.

This unit addresses the Literacy Strategy:
Term 1 objective   1: to compare a range of story settings, and to select words and phrases that describe scenes.

YEAR **3** | UNIT **1** | Sheet **A**   Name _____   Story Settings

Carefully read the following two story beginnings.

The Nightmare Summer

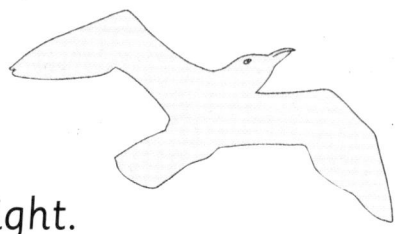

Today was the best day of the holiday so far. The shimmering sand had burnt our bare feet, it had been so hot, and we had hopped from foot to foot, screaming with delight.

Gill had found two starfish, pink and half-hidden under the rocks. In the piles of smelly seaweed and twisted driftwood, I had found hundreds of little crabs scuttling back and forth.

After lunch, I had sat watching the screaming gulls swoop and dive over the pier that stuck out into the sea, like the long arm of some giant swimmer.

The sea had been flat and calm all day, and we kids had made the most of it, tumbling in and out of the warm water. Robert had managed to swim two strokes without his armbands on and had jumped round our little camp of deckchairs and picnic things in his excitement.

This really had been a perfect day.

The start of the story sounds really pleasant but, the title suggests that something is going to go wrong. Perhaps you would like to continue the story showing how things turn out rather badly.

Green Street

The alley was the quickest route back to the flats, but Sol always dreaded those fear-filled minutes it took to get from one end to the other. The overflowing bags and boxes of mysterious rubbish spilt over the path, and Sol picked his way through, taking care with every step.

The blue gate of number 7, with its peeling paint, screeched as he scrambled past. In the gloom, Sol could make out the gaping, black hole that was number 21.

Sol hated this part of the alleyway the most, as there was no door and he could see clearly into the tangled, overgrown garden. There were so many places that things could be hiding. He had often thought he had heard noises coming out of the thick jungle.

As he hurried past, a thin, tabby cat vanished into the dense mat of blackberries and stinging nettles, searching for its dinner. Sol shivered and walked on.

Name _____   Story Settings

1. Match the story to its correct setting by drawing a line to it.

at school

in hospital

in an alleyway

The Nightmare Summer

on a farm

at the seaside

Green Street

by a river

in a supermarket

2. Which words tell us about the setting?
    Write four words or phrases from each extract that give us clues about
    the setting.

The Nightmare Summer

1. _____

_____

2. _____

_____

3. _____

_____

4. _____

_____

Green Street

1. _____

_____

2. _____

_____

3. _____

_____

4. _____

_____

3. The writer has tried to make a very clear picture in your head, by using vivid adjectives.

Find the words below in the extract called 'Green Street'. Write a different word to replace the underlined adjective.

The word does not have to mean the same as the adjective that it is replacing, but it must still make sense in the text.

'overflowing bags' _____

_____

'mysterious rubbish' _____

_____

'peeling paint' _____

_____

'tangled, overgrown garden' _____

_____

'thin, tabby cat' _____

_____

4. **On the back**

Choose one of the settings to draw. Read your chosen extract again and highlight or underline all the words and phrases that tell you what the setting looks like. Write them in the space below if it helps. Use these details to make your drawing as accurate as possible. When you have drawn your picture, copy some of your highlighted/underlined words or phrases on to your drawing.

Mum's Questions

Read this short conversation.

Who do you think is talking?

"Have you had your shower?" asked Mum.

"Yes, it was a lovely shower," he replied.

"Did you hang your towel up?" asked Mum.

"Yes, of course I did," he replied.

"Did you put your clothes in the wash?"

"Yes."

"Have you cleaned your teeth yet?"

"Yes."

We don't know who Mum is talking to.
Who do you think Mum is talking to?

_____

_____

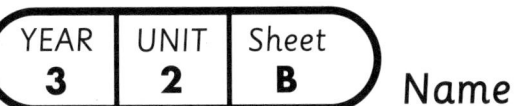

Who is Mum
talking to?

Read the story again to
find out.

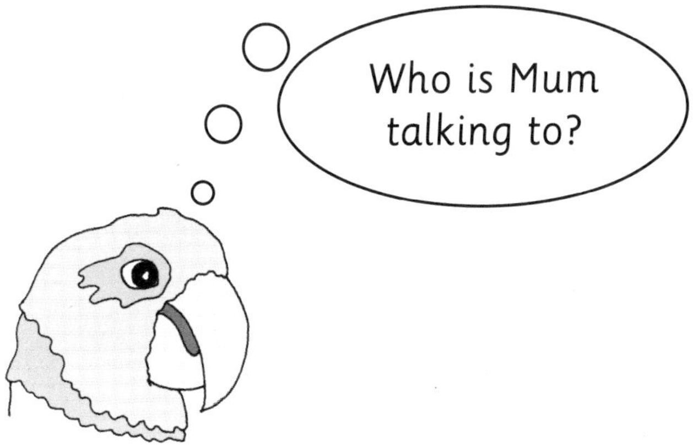

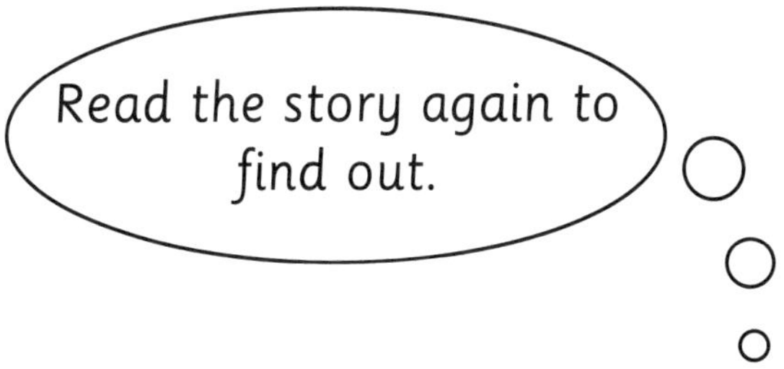

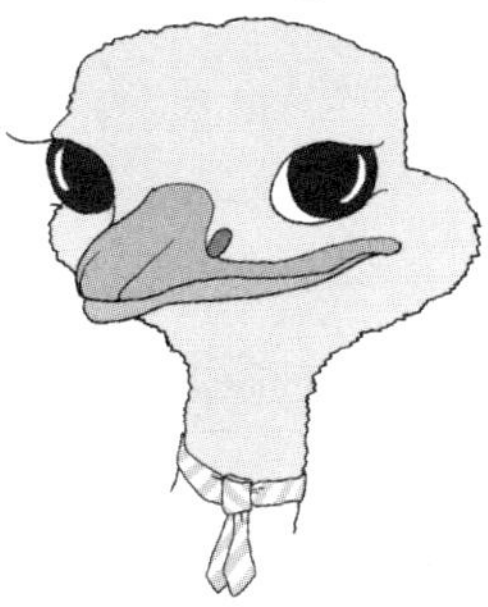

"Have you had your shower?" asked Mum.

"Yes, it was a lovely shower," he replied.

"Did you hang your towel up?" asked Mum.

"Yes, of course I did," he replied.

"Did you put your clothes in the wash?"

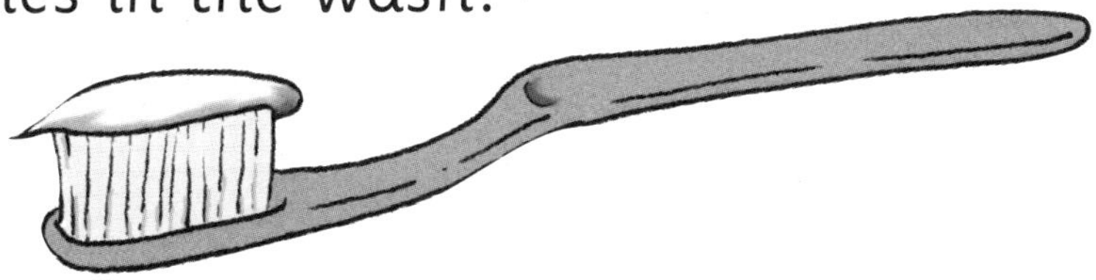

"Yes."

"Have you cleaned your teeth yet?"

"Yes."

"Well done Dad," said Kate.

Who is Mum talking to? [   ]

Is this what you expected? Explain why or why not.

_____

_____

There are three characters altogether. Who are they?

[   ] [   ] [   ]

Here is the story of Mum, Dad and Kate again.

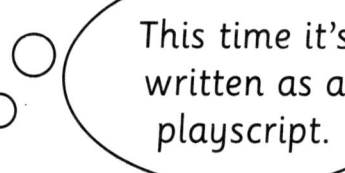

This time it's written as a playscript.

The scene is set in a sitting room. A mother and her daughter, Kate, are watching television. Dad enters, wearing a dressing gown.

Mum: Have you had your shower?

Dad: Yes, it was a lovely shower.

Mum: Did you hang your towel up?

Dad: Yes, of course I did.

Mum: Did you put your clothes in the wash?

Dad: Yes.

Mum: Have you cleaned your teeth?

Dad: Yes.

Kate: Well done Dad.

You could act this scene with some friends.

Name

How Dialogue
is Presented

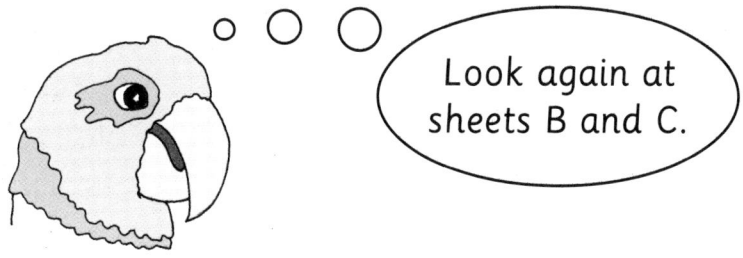

Look again at
sheets B and C.

The story is the same on both sheets but the way it is written is different. The writing on sheet B is called prose. The writing on sheet C is called playscript. Here are some questions to think about.
Talk about the questions with a partner.

Some words are used in the prose but not in the playscript. What are they?

_____

_____

Some punctuation marks are used in the prose but not in the playscript. What are they?

_____

_____

Some punctuation marks are used in the playscript but not in the prose. What are they?

_____

_____

The playscript has some extra sentences. Where do they appear? Why are they there?

_____

_____

_____

Do you prefer the prose or the playscript?

_____

This unit addresses the Literacy Strategy:
Term 1 objective   1: to compare a range of story settings, and to select words and phrases that describe scenes.
Term 1 objective   2: how dialogue is presented in stories, e.g through statements, questions, exclamations; how paragraphing is used to
                        organise dialogue.

YEAR **3** | UNIT **3** | Sheet **A**   **Name** _____   **Little Penguin**

Read this story about two penguins, written by Holly aged 9.

Little Penguin

Little Penguin climbed out of the sea onto the iceberg. He climbed up and up to the shelf of ice where his igloo was. Little Penguin went inside the igloo through a very short tunnel and sat down on a blanket. He put on a green and blue T-shirt which was stripy and spotty, the same as the blanket, and then waddled further up the iceberg to where his best friend lived on another shelf of ice in an igloo.

"Do you want to sail right round this igloo with me?" Little Penguin asked his friend.

"Ooh yes please!" his friend said. So they both climbed down the iceberg to where Little Penguin's boat was, and where the sea was lapping against the side. They both climbed into the wooden boat and untied the mooring rope. The penguins took an oar each and began to row, slowly, round the iceberg. There were lots of other icebergs dotted here and there in the cool bluey-green sea.

All the way round they could see the lighthouse, at the very top of the biggest iceberg, that shone a bright light all day and all night to warn ships there were icebergs nearby.

When the penguins had gone right round the icebergs and were back where they started, they decided to go swimming in the swimming pool. They took their T-shirts off and put them by the side of the pool.

Then together they jumped into the cool water of the swimming pool which was surrounded with a sparkling wall of ice. The two penguins had a great time in the pool, dipping, diving, swimming and gliding.

Basic Comprehension

Where does Little Penguin live?

_____

What colour was Little Penguin's T-shirt?

_____

When Little Penguin and his friend climbed into the boat, what was
the first thing they did? _____

_____

What was on the top of the biggest iceberg?

_____

What are lighthouses for?

_____

_____

What question did Little Penguin ask his friend? Copy the question
out including the speech marks and question mark.

_____

_____

What was his friend's reply? Copy the reply out in full including the
speech marks and exclamation mark.

_____

_____

Layout of Speech.

Look back at the story and see how the spoken parts are written
with speech marks **around what is actually spoken**. A
new line is started when someone speaks.

ADJECTIVES

Adjectives are describing words. For each of the nouns below add 2 more adjectives of your own. Make them as interesting as you can.

sparkling

enormous

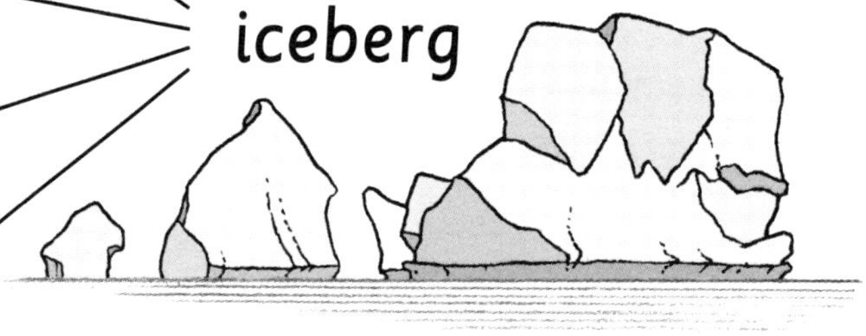

iceberg

star-filled

thundery

sky

rippling

wavy

sea

Put the following statements in the correct order.

☐ Little Penguin asked his friend if he wanted to go out in the boat.

☐ They went for a swim.

☐ Little Penguin went inside his igloo through a tunnel.

☐ Little Penguin and his friend took off their T-shirts.

☐ They saw the lighthouse at the top of the iceberg.

☐ He put on his T-shirt.

Write a short conversation between two characters. Use speech marks to show what is being said. Look back at the story of "Little Penguin" to show how it should be set out. You could write another conversation between Little Penguin and his friend if you want to.

_____

_____

_____

_____

_____

_____

_____

_____

_____

_____

_____

This unit addresses the Literacy Strategy:
Term 1 objective   1: to compare a range of story settings, and to select words and phrases that describe scenes.
Term 1 objective   2: how dialogue is presented in stories, e.g through statements, questions, exclamations; how paragraphing is used to organise dialogue.
Term 1 objective   4: to read, prepare and present playscripts.
Term 1 objective   5: to recognise the key differences between prose and playscript, e.g. by looking at dialogue, stage directions, layout of text in prose and playscripts.

YEAR	UNIT	Sheet
3	4	A

Name

King Midas

King Midas

King Midas lived in Greece, a long time ago. One day, an old man came to his palace. He was lost and had been found wandering near the palace. King Midas took care of him, giving him food, drink and somewhere to sleep. After twelve days, the old man told King Midas that he could grant him a wish to reward him for his kindness. King Midas thought and thought and finally he wished that everything he touched would turn to gold. The old man sighed and told him that this was not a good wish, but if that was what he really wanted then he would grant his wish.

"Yes, yes, I love everything that is gold!" cried King Midas.

With that, the old man disappeared.

Midas stretched out his hand and touched a leaf on a tree. As he did so, it changed from a soft, living leaf to a stiff, heavy, glittering, gold leaf. Midas was so excited and ran to find his wife and daughter.

"I have amazing news!" he cried. "Bring me food and wine, we must celebrate."

As he put the wine to his mouth, it turned to gold and the ham glittered in his hand before he could eat it. The Queen and Princess were amazed to see the food turn to gold. King Midas quickly explained about the old man.

Helena reached out to hold her father's hand. The girl instantly turned into a solid, golden statue. The King and Queen stared in amazement at their only daughter. Bitterly, they wept, when they realised that no longer would they hear her lovely voice, or see her run through the palace.

In the next few days, no one would come near the King for fear of being turned into gold. Even the Queen would not go near him. The King could not eat or drink and even his bed had turned to hard, cold gold. King Midas knew that he must find the old man and ask him to take the wish away.

The King travelled throughout his country for a year and a day and finally found the old man in a hut, high in the mountains. King Midas begged the old man to take back the wish. The old man saw that Midas had suffered greatly, and agreed to take back the wish. Midas hurried home to his palace, where his wife and daughter were waiting for him. All that he had turned to gold had become itself again.

Midas knew his wish had been a foolish one and was glad that, once again, he could feel living things.

King Midas (Playscript)

The Characters

King Midas
Old man
Queen
Princess Helena
Servant

The scene is set in Ancient Greece. King Midas is in his bedroom at the palace. A servant comes in with an old man.

SCENE 1

Servant   *(Bowing to the King.)* My Lord, this old man has been found wandering by the palace gates. He is tired and hungry.

King Midas   Come in, old man, and take some rest.

Old Man   That is very kind of you, sir.

    (The old man sits on a chair.)

King Midas   Do not worry, we will take care of you and treat you well. Old people are very welcome in this palace.

Old Man   You are too kind, sir.

SCENE 2

12 days later, the old man looks stronger and healthier and is about to leave the palace.

Old Man   You have been very kind to me and I want to reward you for your kindness. I have it in my power to grant you one wish. You may wish for anything you want.

King Midas   Oh, goodness me, what shall I wish for? *(Talking to himself.)* Perhaps I should wish for another palace. But no, what would I do with two palaces? I know, I'll ask for a golden coach. No, wait, I have a better idea. *(He turns to talk to the old man.)* I wish that all I touch turns to gold.

Old Man   Are you sure sir? That is not a very wise wish.

King Midas   Yes, yes, I love everything that is gold.

Old Man   Very well, your wish is granted. *(The old man disappears.)*

King Midas   *(To himself.)* Well, how strange, I don't feel any different. What shall I touch first? This leaf will do. *(He touches the leaf and it turns to gold.)* Golly gosh, my stars! It really is. I must hurry home and tell my wife and daughter Helena about this.

SCENE 3

The King rushes into the sitting room where his wife and Helena are sewing busily.

King Midas I have amazing news. Something so strange has happened.

(*To servant*) Bring me food and wine, we must celebrate.

Helena What is this news, papa? Do tell us.

Queen Yes dear, what are you so excited about?

The servant brings in the food and the wine.

With a partner, finish writing the playscript for the story of King Midas.
You need to use the back of this sheet to write on as well.

Playscripts and stories are written down in different ways. Here is a list of some of the differences. Sort them into two lists by writing the numbers in the correct columns. Some of the sentences may fit into both lists.

1 | It has a list of all the character's names.

2 | When people speak, there are speech marks round what they say.

3 | The person who is speaking has their name at the start of the line.

4 | The characters are told where to move to and what they must do.

5 | It is written in paragraphs.

6 | It describes where the story is happening.

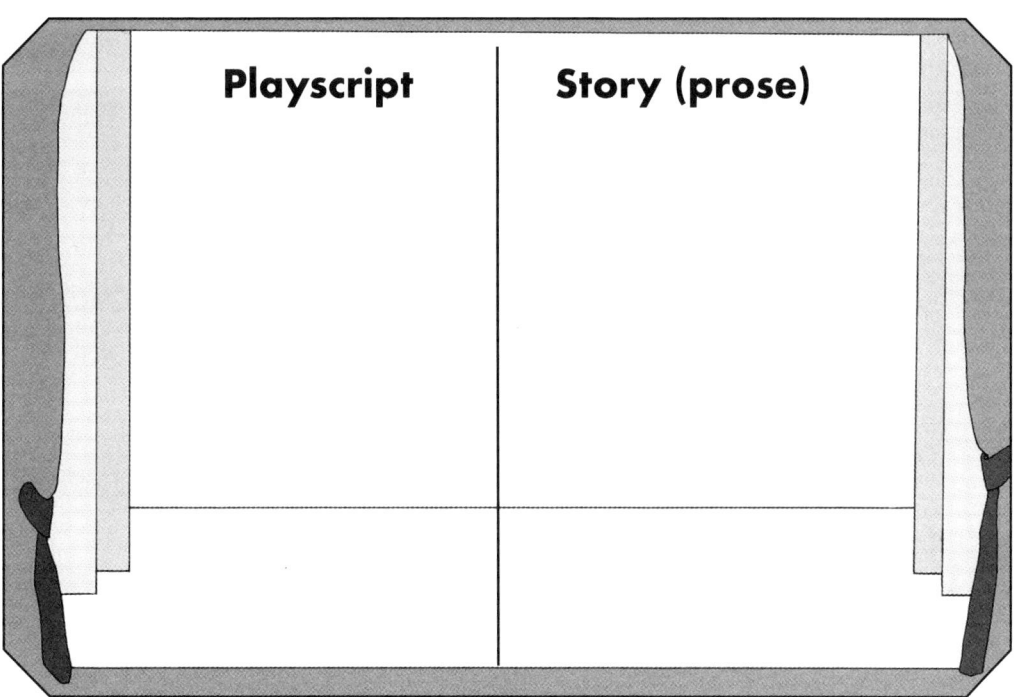

Playscript	Story (prose)

The words written in *italics* in the playscript are to set the scene or to tell the actors where to move to or what to do. Look at the playscript and find some of the words in *italics*. Copy some of them down here.

_____

_____

_____

_____

This unit addresses the Literacy Strategy:
Term 1 objective   6: to read aloud and recite poems, comparing different views of the same subject, to discuss choice of words and phrases that
                        describe and create impact, e.g. adjectives, powerful and expressive verbs, e.g. 'stare' instead of 'look'.
Term 1 objective   7: to distinguish between rhyming and non-rhyming poetry and comment on the impact of layout.
Term 2 objective   4: to choose and prepare poems for performance, identifying appropriate expression, tone, volume and use of voices and other
                        sounds.
Term 2 objective   5: rehearse and improve performance, taking note of punctuation and meaning.
Term 3 objective   7: to select, prepare, read aloud and recite by heart poetry that plays with language or entertains; to recognise rhyme,
                        alliteration and other patterns of sound that create effects.

Plane Poems

Looking Down

Seeing the scene from way up high:
Roads and fields, turrets and spires,
All set out like a story book,
To be admired by countless flyers.

Miniature boats on picture-book seas,
Coastal strips of yellow sand,
Fluffy patches of cotton wool clouds,
Casting shadows on bright clear land.

Beyond the fields, above the slopes,
Mountain ranges, glinting white,
Bathed in sunlight fresh and new.
A privilege to see this sight.

The changing views by day and night,
Quite magical from up so high.
The world in its true glory
Can be seen from in the sky.

First Flight

Approaching the airport
Apprehensive

Through the departures
Thoughtful

Fastening seat-belts
Fearful

Waiting for take off
Worried

Speeding down runway
Spectacular

Bursting through clouds
Brilliant

A panorama below
Amazing

Descending again
Disappointed

Back down to earth
Bumpy

Slowing down now
Sad

Should do this again
Soon.

Train Poems

From a Railway Carriage

Faster than fairies, faster than witches,
Bridges and houses, hedges and ditches;
And charging along like troops in a battle,
All through the meadows the horses and cattle:

All of the sights of the hill and the plain
Fly as thick as the driving rain;
And ever again, in the wink of an eye,
Painted stations whistle by.

Here is a child who clambers and scrambles,
All by himself and gathering brambles;
Here is a tramp who stands and gazes;
And there is the green for stringing the daisies!

Here is a cart run away in the road
Lumping along with man and load;
And here is a mill, and there is a river:
Each a glimpse and gone for ever!

Robert Louis Stevenson (1850-1894)

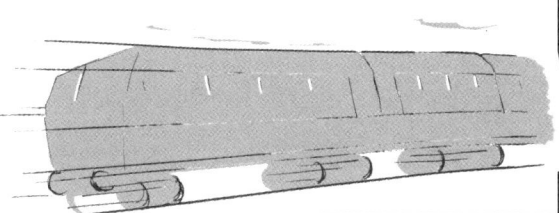

Travel by Train

Clickety clack
The wheels on the track
Rumble along
Singing their song
Faster and faster
Leaving the station
Taking the people
Across the nation.
Rushing with speed
Past field and farm
Shooting through tunnels
Sound the alarm.
Begin to slow down
Approaching the town
Arriving back
Clickety clack.

Plane and Train Poems

Before you answer any questions read each of the four poems aloud.

1. Which poem do you like best? _____

2. Why do you like it best? _____
   _____

3. Which poem was written by Robert Louis Stevenson?
   _____

4. Which of the four poems does not use a rhyming pattern?
   _____

5. Which word in the poem 'Looking Down' means the same as **very small**? _____

6. In the last verse of 'From a Railway Carriage', which word tells you that the road is bumpy? _____

7. In the poem 'Looking Down', name the words that are rhymed with:-

   (spires) _____   (sand) _____

   (white) _____   (sky) _____

8a. In 'First Flight' did the passenger enjoy the flight? _____

b. How do you know this? _____
   _____
   _____

9. In 'First Flight', what does the word **descending** mean? _____

On the back of the sheet use your best writing to copy out your favourite poem. Practise reading it aloud.

Name   **Plane and
Train Poems**

Advanced Comprehension

10. Which two poems make use of rhythm to create an effect?

_____   _____

11. Why do you think the poets used rhythm?

_____

_____

12. Which poem uses alliteration? _____

13. Which of the following words means the nearest to the word
     apprehensive? Ring the correct answer.

(**happy**)   (**anxious**)   (**terrified**)   (**arriving**)

14. In 'From a Railway Carriage' why do you think
     the poet chose the word **charging** in verse one? _____

     _____

15. Can you suggest another word that could have been used instead of
     shooting in 'Travel by Train'? _____

16. Write a definition for the word **panorama** used in 'First Flight'. You
     may need a dictionary to help you.

     _____

     _____

17. Work with a partner to prepare one of the poems to perform. See if
     you can learn the poem by heart. Follow the punctuation, and use the
     important words and the rhythm to help your performance.

Extra Activities

Either Read 'First Flight'. Pretend you are the passenger getting on
     the plane for your first flight and use the information in the poem to
     write a short story about what happened and how your feelings
     changed.

Or   Write a poem of your own about travelling on some sort of vehicle.
     Think about whether you will use rhyme, or layout, or rhythm or
     some other way to make your poem effective.

This unit addresses the Literacy Strategy:
Term 1 objective   16: to understand the distinction between fact and fiction; to use terms 'fact', 'fiction' and 'non-fiction' appropriately.
Term 1 objective   17: to notice differences in the style and structure of fiction and non-fiction writing.
Term 1 objective   18: to locate information, using contents, index, headings, sub-headings, page numbers, bibliographies.
Term 1 objective   19: to compare the way information is presented, e.g. by comparing a variety of information texts including IT-based sources.
Term 1 objective   20: to read information passages, and identify main points or gist of text, e.g. by noting or underlining key words or phrases, listing the four or five key points covered.

Little Owl

The Little Owl is the smallest species of owl found in Britain. When it is fully grown its height is only 22cm.

It is an unusual owl because it appears in the daytime - most owls are nocturnal.

It eats worms and insects such as beetles, earwigs and crane-flies.

The Little Owl makes its nest in a barn or in an old tree. The female usually lays between three and five eggs then keeps them warm for about four weeks. Both adults look after the young. The nestlings fly approximately five weeks after hatching.

In the winter, Little Owls sometimes live in old rabbit holes.

This passage tells us some **facts.**

Writing that presents us with facts is called **non-fiction.**

Read the passage about the Little Owl...

...then answer these questions.

1. Why is the Little Owl unusual?

    _____

    _____

2. Where does the Little Owl make its nest?

    _____

    _____

3. How many eggs does the Little Owl lay?

    _____

    _____

4. What do Little Owls eat?

    _____

    _____

Look in the library for books about birds.

5. Can you find the names of some other owls that live in our country?

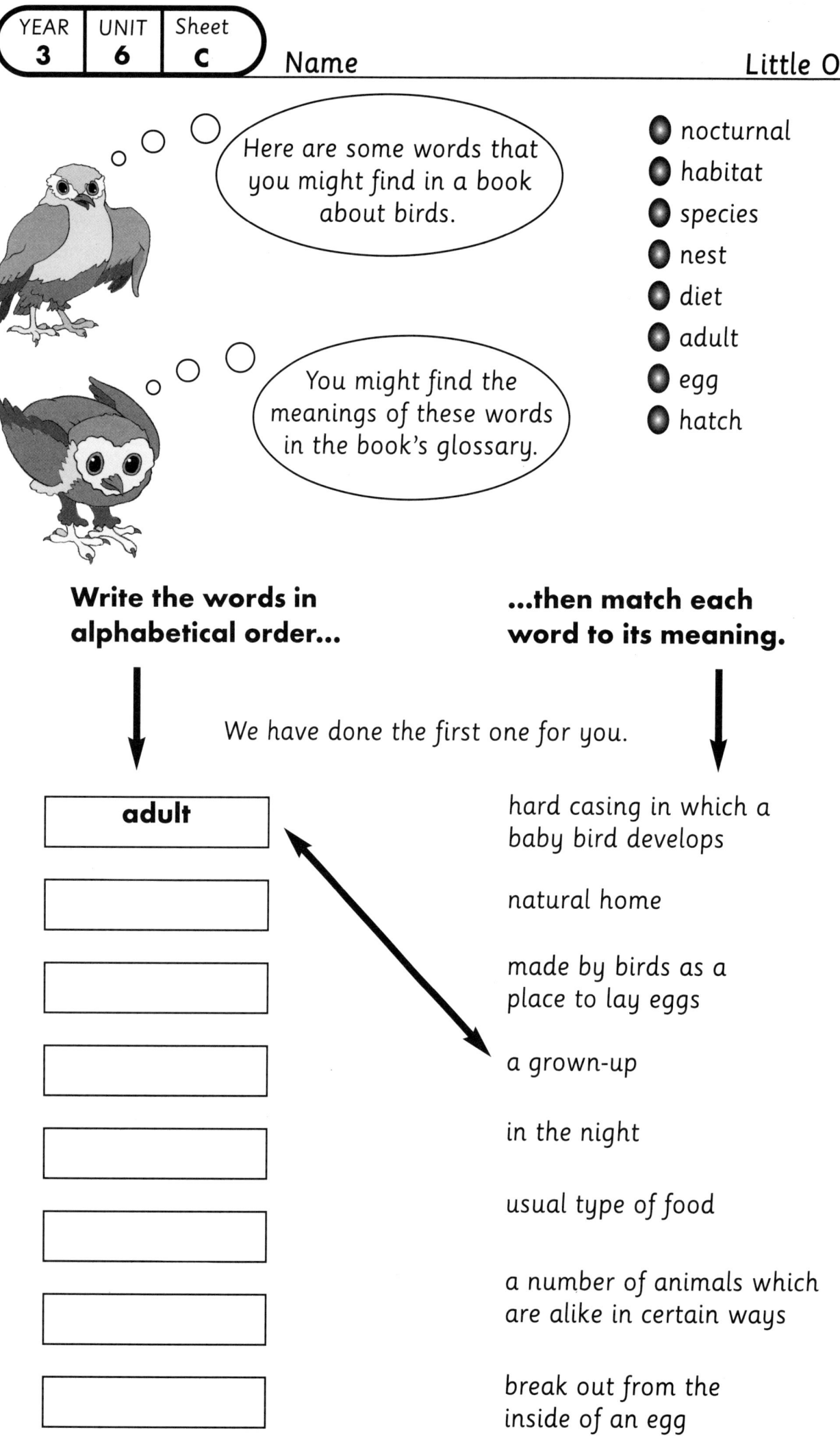

Here are some words that you might find in a book about birds.

You might find the meanings of these words in the book's glossary.

- nocturnal
- habitat
- species
- nest
- diet
- adult
- egg
- hatch

Write the words in alphabetical order...

...then match each word to its meaning.

We have done the first one for you.

adult

hard casing in which a baby bird develops

natural home

made by birds as a place to lay eggs

a grown-up

in the night

usual type of food

a number of animals which are alike in certain ways

break out from the inside of an egg

YEAR 3 | UNIT 6 | Sheet D

Name ____________________ Little Owl

Here are the names of some birds.

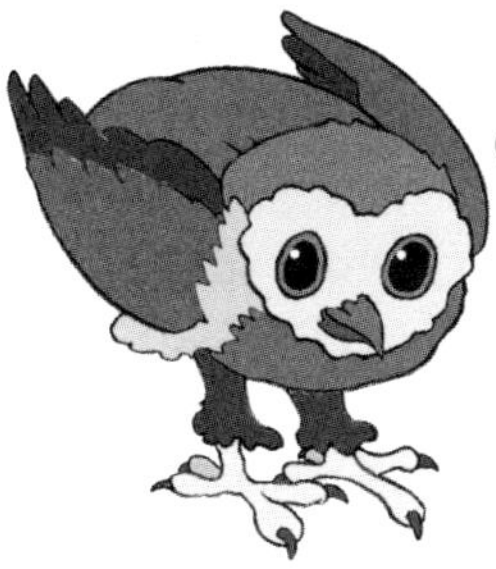

Write the names out in alphabetical order.

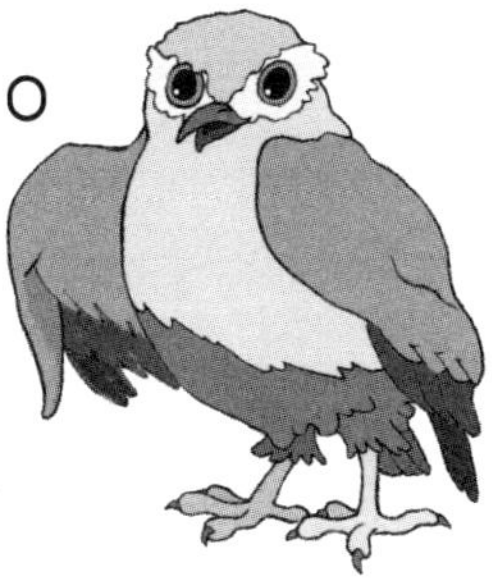

swan sparrow

robin eagle coot blackbird

wren pheasant dipper

starling lark swallow

Remember: you may need to look at the second or third letter to put the name in the right place.

Choose one of the birds and use a book to find out about it.

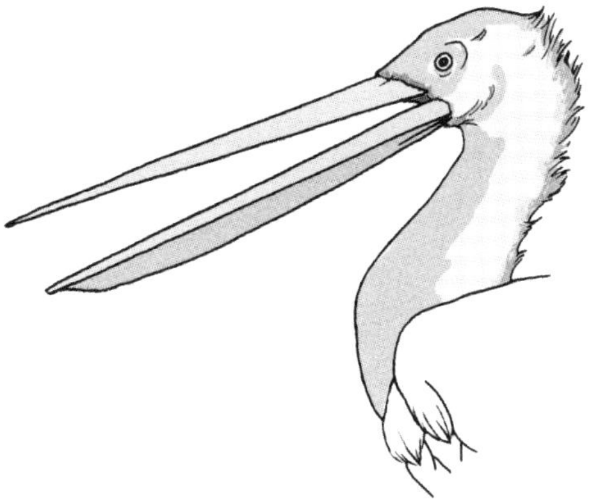

Write about the bird, using these headings:

Appearance

Diet

Habitat

Number of eggs

This unit addresses the Literacy Strategy:
Term 1 objective 16: to understand the distinction between fact and fiction; to use terms 'fact', 'fiction' and non-fiction' appropriately.
Term 1 objective 17: to notice differences in the style and structure of fiction and non-fiction writing.

YEAR	UNIT	Sheet
3	7	A

Name   Fact and Fiction

Which of these book titles are more likely to be non-fiction, and which fiction? Write either **fact** or **fiction** under each title.

Spooky Nights and Weird Wizards	Adventures of Buzzman ZZZZ	SPLAT Goes to Town
....	....	....
Crazy Animals to Make With Paper	Where Does Cheese Come From?	New Computer Games
....	....	....

1. Three of these words or phrases mean the same as **non-fiction**.
   Tick the boxes next to the words or phrases.

   something that is going to happen ☐   fact ☐

   true information ☐   an adventure ☐

   something that has actually happened ☐

2. Three of these words or phrases mean the same as **fiction**.
   Tick the boxes next to the words or phrases.

   a story ☐   a newspaper report ☐   make believe ☐

   something made up ☐   information about something real ☐

page 1

CONTENTS

page 2

Sarah loved to curl up in a tight ball under the kitchen table. In this quiet haven, she could think about the strange dreams that she was having each night. She remembered the shining man who had seemed so real. She wondered about the things he had told her.

page 3

RIVERS

<u>The Nile</u>
The River Nile runs through Egypt. It is very important to Egyptian people as they use it for many things.
They wash and clean their clothes in it. They water their fields with its water and use it for many other things. There are stories about the Egyptian gods and the River Nile.

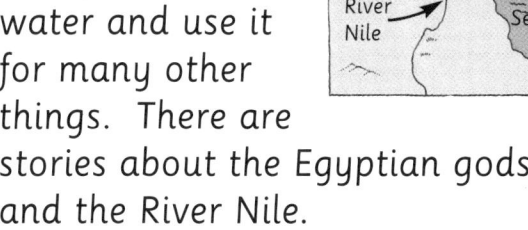

<u>The Amazon</u>
The Amazon runs through.....

page 4

Nick and Joe rubbed their eyes. How could this be happening? Pirate ships were only in story books, yet they were on the wide open sea with a bunch of dangerous cut-throat pirates coming towards them. One minute they had been in the antique shop, looking at that dusty old book and now....

1. Which two pages have got characters in them? _____ and _____

2. Which page has got a title and sub-headings? _____

3. Which pages have got interesting stories? _____ and _____

4.   Which page tells us where to find more information?   _____

5.   Which page has a drawing which gives more information?   _____

6.   Which pages are from fiction books and which are from non-fiction books? Explain how you know this by filling in the spaces below.

Page 1. I know this is from a non-fiction/fiction book because

_____

Page 2. I know this is from a non-fiction/fiction book because

_____

Page 3. I know this is from a non-fiction/fiction book because

_____

Page 4. I know this is from a non-fiction/fiction book because

_____

7.a. Read the statements below. Do you believe they are true?
      Put a tick in the box if you think that the statement is true.

1. A puppy is a young dog.   ☐

2. The dog jumped 25 metres into the air.   ☐

3. A dog can run faster than a snail.   ☐

4. The dog grew another leg behind its ear.   ☐

b. Remember that fiction books contain stories that are made up - they are not true. **Non-fiction books contain true facts**. Which of the statements above could be in a **non-fiction** book?

_____

_____

A fact is something that has actually happened, whereas an **opinion** is what someone thinks about something. Read the letter on the next page carefully and then decide which of it is fact and which opinion.

Dear Ada,

What do you think of all these new computers that seem to be everywhere? They have changed the way we all live. I see them in supermarkets, schools, libraries and many businesses. Most children have got them in their homes. Children these days spend more time using the computer than doing anything else. I hardly ever see them playing with a ball. I know that computers do have their uses, and can be used to send messages to the other side of the world by e-mail, but people have stopped writing ordinary letters to each other, which is such a shame.

With love

John

8.   a. List 3 facts in this text:

1. _____

2. _____

3. _____

b. List 3 opinions in this text:

1. _____

2. _____

3. _____

9.   Look at each statement below. Is it fact or opinion?
Draw a line under the correct word.

Football is great fun.   FACT/OPINION

Football is played with a ball.   FACT/OPINION

England has a football team.   FACT/OPINION

England's football team is the best in the world.   FACT/OPINION

In the game of football, there is a goal at each end of the pitch.
FACT/OPINION

Read the following information written by a class teacher to his class.

Class Trip to
Willow Marsh Nature Reserve

Date of trip: - Wednesday 21st June
Times: - leave school 9.15am
                      - return 4pm

This year our class trip will be to the Willow Marsh Nature Reserve. The coach will leave school at 9.15am promptly and we are expected to arrive at the Reserve at 10.30am.

Mrs Ann Green will be our guide for the day. We hope to see herons nesting, a variety of small birds and learn about the habitat of the animals that live in the Reserve, for example, badgers, rabbits, stoats and foxes.

You will need to bring:

☆ wellington boots or waterproof shoes in a bag
☆ a waterproof jacket in case of rain (also useful to sit on)
☆ a packed lunch with plenty to drink
☆ no more than £2 to spend in the small shop

It is not necessary to wear school uniform. I would suggest old clothes, such as trousers, to protect your legs from stinging nettles, t-shirt, jumper and trainers.

A clip board will be provided.

A donation of £5 towards the cost of the trip would be appreciated.

Please show this information to your parents, or the adults who look after you, and ask them to fill in the form below if you are able to go. Please return it to school by Friday.

Mr Samways
Class teacher

✂ -

I would like (child's name)......................................to go on the trip to Willow Marsh Nature Reserve on Wed. 21st June.

I enclose a donation of £5 towards the cost of the trip. ☐

Signed:..parent or guardian.

Basic Comprehension

▮ Use a highlighter pen (or underline) to select the most important facts that Mr Samways wrote in his letter to his class.

▮ List the main points below:-

1. _____

2. _____

3. _____

4. _____

▮ What are the 2 things that you could use a waterproof jacket for?

1. _____

2. _____

▮ What does Mr Samways hope the children will learn on their trip?

_____

_____

_____

▮ Who should fill in the form at the end of the information sheet?

_____

▮ What else could be returned to school with the form?

_____

▮ Why do you think Mr Samways used bullet points when he was writing about what the children should bring on the trip?

_____

_____

Use the frame below to write an invitation to a friend to come on a birthday treat with you. Include the date, time and where you will be going. It could be to the park to play football, to the cinema, to a local museum or for a picnic. You can choose, but make sure your friend has all the information he or she needs.

If you were going on a class trip, where would you choose to go? Try to explain why you would like to go there.

_____

_____

_____

What do you think your class would learn by going on the trip you have chosen?

_____

_____

_____

If you had to write a letter inviting your class on your trip, what would you tell the children they had to bring with them?

1. _____

2. _____

3. _____

4. _____

What would be the best time of year to go on your trip or does it not matter? Can you explain why?

_____

_____

How many adults would you need to help with your trip?

_____

As well as your class teacher, which adults would you take?

_____

_____

This unit addresses the Literacy Strategy:
Term 1 objective 17: to notice differences in the style and structure of fiction and non-fiction writing.
Term 1 objective 18: to locate information, using contents, index, headings, sub-headings, page numbers, bibliographies.
Term 1 objective 19: to compare the way information is presented, e.g. by comparing a variety of information texts including IT-based sources.

YEAR **3** | UNIT **9** | Sheet **A**   Name   Swans

SWANS

Swans are large aquatic birds. They are usually white in colour, though black swans are also found. They have long necks, and their feet are webbed to help in swimming. Whilst there are several species of swan, the one most commonly found in British lakes and waterways is the **mute swan**.

A female swan is known as a **pen**, the male is a **cob** and the young swan is a **cygnet**.

History

For many centuries people in Britain enjoyed eating swan meat, which was often a feature of feasts and banquets. The mute swan was used for this purpose, and swan keepers would mark the birds to show who owned them. Any swan that had not been marked became the property of the Crown. For this reason swans have become known as royal birds.

Swans were also valued for their feathers which made good 'quills' for writing and the leathery webbing of their feet which could be used to make purses. Even their wing bones were used, as these made effective whistles.

Nowadays we don't farm swans for their meat and other uses, but we enjoy their tame approachable manner.

Mute Swans

These are the swans most commonly found in Britain. They can be distinguished from other species by their orange coloured bill and their habit of curving their necks when they are resting. Mute swans can live to over twenty years of age, but in the wild it is more common for them to live for about six years. If the swan is annoyed it makes a hissing noise, and if threatened will stand high in the water and beat its wings towards the possible threat. The swan's powerful wings can do even a large creature a lot of damage.

Breeding

Swans usually have their first cygnets when they have reached about three years old.

In spring a pair of swans builds a very large nest and the pen lays several eggs (usually between three and seven) in it, at two day intervals. The eggs hatch about 35 days after the last one has been laid. Whilst the eggs are being kept warm, or incubated, the cob behaves very aggressively towards any possible intruders.

Cygnets

When the eggs first hatch the cygnets are coloured grey and have soft downy feathers. After a few weeks these are replaced by brown feathers. By the time the cygnets are 12 months old their feathers are white.

During the early months the cygnets stay with their parents for protection. Though the pen and cob care for and protect their young during this first year, by the following spring they will drive them away, so that the adults can prepare for their next brood of young.

The year-old cygnets will join other flocks of young swans ready to find partners to lay eggs with when they are old enough. It is particularly important for these young swans to be with a flock during their second summer as they will moult during this time, and so for a few weeks will be unable to fly.

Name _____ Swans

Ring the correct answer.

1. Which term correctly describes the text?

   fiction   **non-fiction**   **poetry**

2. How is the first paragraph written?

   in the past tense   **in the present tense**

   in the future tense

3. In which section would you find out about young swans?

   History   **Mute Swans**   **Breeding**   **Cygnets**

4. What does a mute swan do if it is annoyed?

   hisses   **pecks**   **screeches**   **flaps**

5. What is a male swan called?

   pen   **cob**   **cygnet**   **egg**

---

6. How many eggs might a female swan lay? _____

7. Which sub-heading is at the top of the
   section that tells you about swans in the past?_____

8. What colour are the very youngest cygnets?_____

9. What colour beak does the mute swan have? _____

10. What is a female swan called? _____

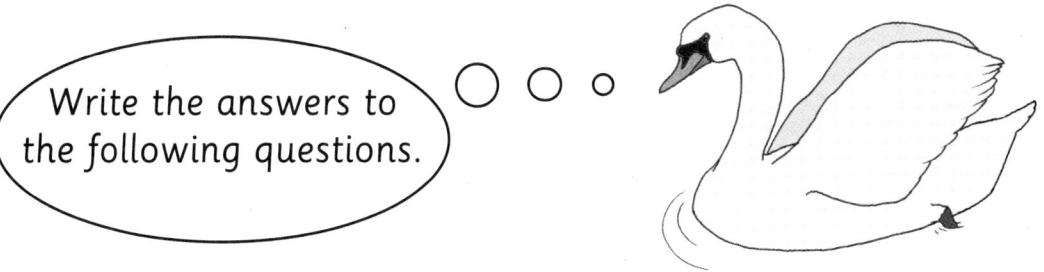

Write the answers to the following questions.

11. There were four reasons that swans were kept in the past. What were these reasons?

_____

_____

12. Most of the text is written in the present tense.
Which section is written in the past tense? _____

13. Write a clear definition for each of the following words taken from the text. You may need a dictionary to help you.

quill _____

_____

banquet _____

webbed feet _____

_____

aquatic _____

_____

moult _____

_____

14. For how long do swans incubate their eggs? _____

15. What are swans unable to do when they are moulting? _____

16. About how old are the cygnets when their parents stop protecting them, and drive them away?

_____

17. On the back of the sheet write five informative sentences about swans in your own words. Include as many important points as possible from the text.

YEAR **3** | UNIT **10** | Sheet **A**   **Name**

The Princess and the Pea

There was once a prince who wanted to marry a princess. He had travelled the world over to find one but he could never be sure that they were real princesses. He returned home and was very sad because he wanted to love a real princess.

Then one evening a terrible storm came on. It thundered and rained and thundered some more. Suddenly a knocking was heard on the castle door. The footman opened the door and found a girl standing there who said she was a princess and would like shelter from the storm. What a sight she was after being in the rain; the water ran from her hair, down her clothes and onto the polished floor of the castle. She did not look like a princess.

The Prince's mother, the Queen, had a plan. She said to the Prince, "We will have a bed made up for the Princess with twenty mattresses. We will put a dried pea under the bottom one and if she feels the pea through all twenty mattresses we will know she is a real princess. Only a real princess could feel something as small as a pea through twenty mattresses."

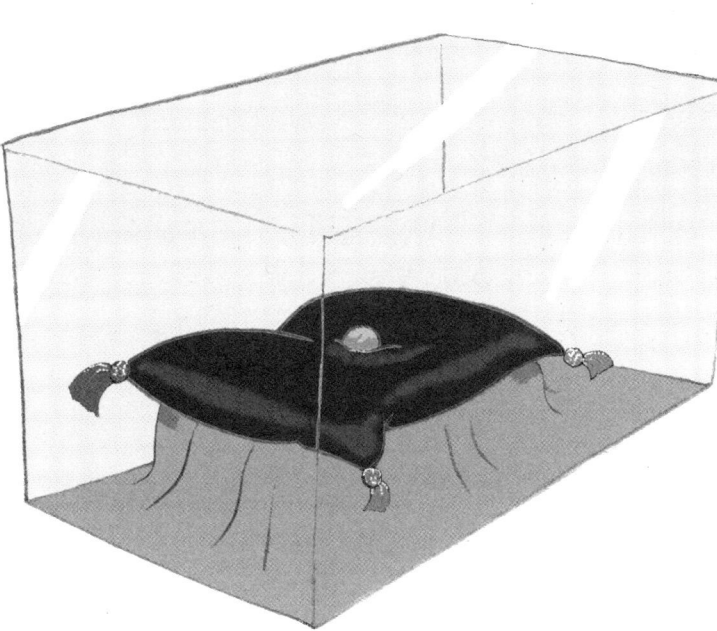

So that was what they did. In the morning the Princess came down for breakfast.

"How did you sleep?" said the Prince.

"Terribly badly," replied the Princess. "Goodness knows what was in the bed but something hard was in my back all night."

Now they knew she was a real princess. The Prince told her what they had done and now the pea is in the Royal Museum. The Prince and the Princess were married and lived happily ever after.

Basic Comprehension

○ Who did the Prince want to marry? _____

○ Where did he look for a bride?

_____

_____

○ Who knocked on the castle door during the storm?

_____

_____

○ What was the Queen's plan to find out if it was a real princess?

_____

_____

_____

_____

This unit addresses the Literacy Strategy:
Term 1 objective 1: to reinforce and apply their word-level skills through shared and guided reading.
Term 1 objective 2: to use phonological, contextual, grammatical and graphic knowledge to work out, predict, and check the meanings of unfamiliar words and to make sense of what they read.
You may also find it helpful when covering :
Term 2 objective 16: to use dictionaries and glossaries to locate words by using initial letter.
Term 3 objective 13: to understand the distinction between fact and fiction; to use terms 'fact', 'fiction' and 'non-fiction' appropriately.

Name

Traditional Stories

The Princess and the Pea is a traditional story. That means it is a very old story that has been retold many times. You may know other traditional tales such as **Aladdin, Jack and the Beanstalk, The Elves and the Shoemaker** or **Sleeping Beauty**. There are many more.

These stories often begin and end in a similar way. Here is a list of beginnings and endings of traditional stories. See if you can find any more to add to the the list by looking at the books in your class or school library.

Traditional Story Beginnings:	
1.	There was once........
2.	A long time ago.......
3.	Close to a large forest there lived........
4.	
5.	

Traditional Story Endings:	
1.	I will never again wander off into the woods.
2.	So all their troubles came to an end and they lived together happily.
3.	And that was the end of the ....
4.	
5.	

○ **On the next page is a writing frame with the start of a story for you to finish. The story is in a traditional style. You could draw a picture to go with your story.**

The Three Wishes

Once upon a time there was a small wooden hut in the middle of a forest. Bobby lived with his family: his mother, his father and his baby sister. They were very, very poor and had to grow their food in the tiny garden in front of the house. They were always hungry and only had the clothes they stood up in.

One day Bobby was playing in the forest with 3 beautiful feathers he had found. Just then a tiny man with a green pointed hat, appeared before him.

"I will give you 3 wishes," said the man, "one for each of those feathers. Give me the feathers and whatever you wish for will come true."

_____

_____

_____

_____

_____

_____

_____

_____

_____

_____

_____

_____

_____

_____

_____

_____

This unit addresses the Literacy Strategy:
Term 2 objective 1: to investigate the styles and <u>voices</u> of traditional story language - collect examples, e.g. story openings and endings; scene openers, e.g. 'Now when...', 'A long time ago...', list, compare and use in own writing.
Term 2 objective 2: to identify typical story themes, e.g. trials and forfeits, good over evil, weak over strong, wise over foolish.
Term 2 objective 3: to identify and discuss main and recurring characters, evaluate their behaviour and justify views.

YEAR	UNIT	Sheet	
3	11	A	Name

The Hare and the Tortoise
- a fable by Aesop. Part 1.

The hare was a very fast runner. He loved to show off about it.

'I can beat you in a race,' he said to the cat.

They had a race and, sure enough, the hare won.

'I can beat you any day,' he said to the dog.

They had a race and, sure enough, the hare won. Soon none of the animals wanted to race with the hare.

'I'm not racing with someone who shows off so much,' said the horse.

Everybody wondered if the horse was scared of losing, but they agreed with him that the hare showed off too much and was very annoying.

'Will you race with me?' The hare asked the rat. 'No, thank you,' said the rat.

The Hare and the Tortoise
- a fable by Aesop. Part 1.

'Will you race with me?' the hare asked the fox.
'No, thank you,' said the fox. The hare asked all the animals. Well, nearly all, because of course he didn't ask the slow ones such as the slug, the snail, the frog, the worm or the tortoise.

'Why don't you ask me?' said the tortoise.
The hare just laughed.
'Why don't you ask me?' said the tortoise again.
This time everybody laughed.
'Why don't you ask me?'
'Tortoise, will you race with me?' said the hare, giggling loudly.
'Yes!' Shouted the tortoise excitedly.

Aesop lived in Greece over two thousand years ago.

He was a slave so he didn't seem to be a very important man.

He made up stories to entertain people.

His stories always had a moral, so they taught people how to behave.

His stories usually had animals as characters. Stories like these are called fables.

We are both characters from Aesop's fables.

Find out about the fables of **The Fox and the Grapes** and **The Goose that Laid Golden Eggs**.

© Andrew Brodie Publications ✓ www.acblack.com

Answer these questions about Aesop.

Write your answers in sentences.

1.   In which country did Aesop live?

   _____

   _____

2.   How long ago did Aesop live?

   _____

   _____

3.   What was special about Aesop's stories?

   _____

   _____

4.   What are stories like this called?

   _____

   _____

5.   Do you think Aesop was an important man? Give reasons for your answer.

   _____

   _____

   _____

This unit addresses the Literacy Strategy:
Term 1 objective   1: to compare a range of story settings, and to select words and phrases that describe scenes.
Term 2 objective   2: to identify typical story themes, e.g. trials and forfeits, good over evil, weak over strong, wise over foolish.
Term 3 objective   2: to refer to significant aspects of the text, e.g. opening, build-up, atmosphere, and to know language is used to create these,
                        e.g. use of adjectives for description.

YEAR **3** | UNIT **12** | Sheet **A**   **Name**   The Ugly Duckling

The Ugly Duckling

It was a bright warm spring day when mother duck heard the shell cracking on her very last egg. The other eggs had hatched days ago and she had begun to think that the last one never would. Some of her friends had already made rather unpleasant remarks about the last egg. It was indeed somewhat larger than all the others, and she couldn't actually remember laying it, but still, she thought, an egg is an egg, and you must look after it until it hatches.

The cracking of the last egg would complete her rather beautiful family of small, soft, fluffy, yellow and brown ducklings. To her amazement her final baby looked strangely different from his brothers and sisters. He was much larger, coloured grey and was rather ungainly. Nonetheless thought mother duck, he is my duckling and I love him just as much as his brothers and sisters, and indeed she did.

The very next day mother duck took her new family to be inspected by the oldest and most respected duck in the farmyard. The wise old duck looked very carefully at each young member of the family. At last she looked up and said, "What a very fine brood you have my dear. It's just a shame about the youngest. He looks like no duck that I have ever seen. It might have been better if he had never hatched."

At that mother duck blushed with embarrassment, and replied, "He may be an unusual little chap, but I'm sure he will eventually make a very fine duck."

Thus began a very miserable year for the newest duckling. He was painfully aware of how he differed from his siblings, and they teased him relentlessly. Other broods of ducklings too were unkind to him, they would creep up from behind and peck him, or call him nasty names. Mother duck, though very well intentioned, couldn't be there to protect him all the time.

The Ugly Duckling felt very frightened and lonely.

At last he could stand it no longer, and one day decided that perhaps he could find friends outside the farmyard. Maybe he could even find other ducklings that looked more like him than his own brothers and sisters.

He flew over the farmyard fence and went as far as his legs and wings would take him.

At the end of the day, as darkness fell, the weary duckling slept, not knowing, or for that matter caring, where he was.

In fact the Ugly Duckling had reached the moors where some wild geese lived. They thought that his appearance was strange, but they kindly offered him a place with them. Unfortunately for the duckling, it was the hunting season, and later that day he heard shots from a gun, as many of his new acquaintances were shot.

"Oh dear," said the Ugly Duckling to himself, "this is not the place for me," as he lay still, too frightened too move. When he was quite sure that the hunters had gone he crept sadly away.

The following day the Ugly Duckling came across a small, and rather ramshackle cottage. Here there lived an old woman with her cat and her hen. The cat would curl up on the woman's lap and keep her company, and the hen would lay a fresh egg for her breakfast each day.

When the Ugly Duckling arrived, the cat immediately asked how he thought he could possibly be of any use to the household. The old lady was a little kinder, and thought that this rather strange little duck, like the hen, might be able to lay her an egg each day. Of course being a male this was quite impossible, so a few weeks later the Ugly Duckling was homeless once more.

During the final weeks of the summer the Ugly Duckling kept himself to himself for fear of rejection.

One day he saw some magnificent white birds flying above him. He didn't know what they were, but something about them held his attention. He thought these great white birds, with their elegant long necks and their huge white wings, were the most wonderful things he had ever seen.

How lucky they were he thought, to be beautiful, and not to know the suffering he had endured through being so ugly.

Autumn turned to winter, and it was the most cold and miserable time imaginable for the duckling. The very worst time was when even the water froze around him and he had nowhere to swim and difficulty finding food and drink.

Eventually, after what seemed like an eternity, the duckling became aware that spring was on its way. The sun had some warmth in it and there was the gentle hum of insects around him in the air. He stepped carefully into the water that morning, then he heard the shout of a young child: "Mum, Dad, quickly come and look, there is a new swan on the river today!"

The Ugly Duckling wondered where the swan could be. The child was looking down the river in his direction, yet when he turned his head he saw nothing behind him. He soon saw that the child was holding a piece of bread, and being very hungry he decided to risk swimming towards her.

The girl fed the Ugly Duckling from the river bank, all the while talking to her parents about the beautiful swan she was feeding.

A few minutes later a whole group of fabulous white birds, came regally along the river from the other direction. He recognised these as the birds he had seen and envied the previous summer.

"Oh look," said the girl on the river bank excitedly, "here are the rest of the swans!"

The Ugly Duckling was both intrigued and alarmed by the arrival of the swans. Intrigued by their beauty and grace and alarmed by how they might react to him.

The largest and most handsome of the swans called to him in welcome, asking him to join their group.

"But why ever would you want an ugly duckling like me to join you?" he asked.

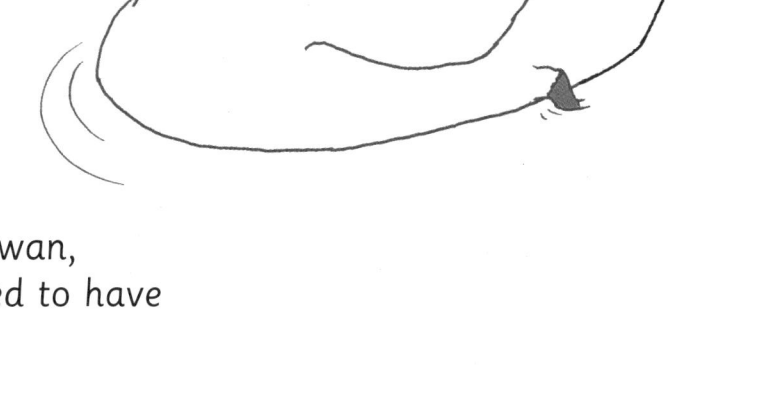

"A duckling!" chuckled the largest swan. "Why ever would you think you are a duckling? Look at your reflection in the water: you are an exceedingly fine looking swan, and we would be honoured to have you join us."

It was the most wonderful moment for the swan (for as you will have guessed that is of course what he was). He looked into the clear water, and saw, looking back at him, a large and very handsome swan with an elegant neck and fine strong white wings.

Never again was he unhappy or lonely. From that day on he joined his new friends and lived a happier life than he had ever imagined possible.

Ring the correct answers. ○ ○ ○

○ Which word in paragraph one is used to describe the remarks made about the last egg?

unkind   **unfortunate**   **unpleasant**   **unseen**

○ How are the yellow and brown ducklings described?

shiny, small, soft   **soft, fine, fluffy**

small, soft, fluffy   **small, silly, fluffy**

○ Where did the Ugly Duckling meet some geese?

across the fields   **near a lake**   **on the moors**

○ Which of the following words is nearest in meaning to **ramshackle**?

small   **old**   **rented**   **rickety**

○ What did the 'old woman' hope the duck could do for her?

quack   **lay eggs**   **sit on her lap**

Write the correct answers. ○ ○ ○

○ Why couldn't the Ugly Duckling lay eggs?

_____

○ At the end of the story what did the Ugly Duckling see when he looked into the clear water? _____

_____

○ Write four of the adjectives used in the story to describe the swan.

_____

○ **On the back of the sheet draw and colour a picture of one scene from the story.**

Advanced Comprehension

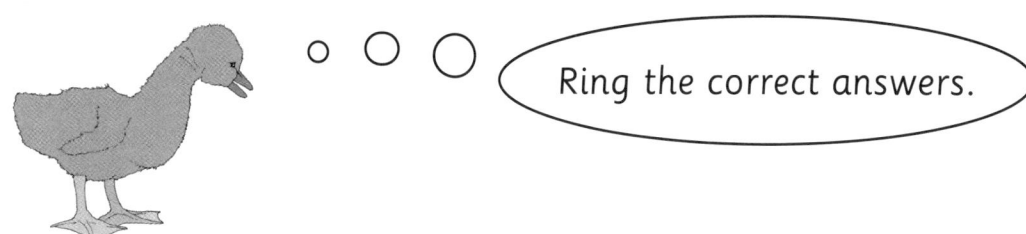

Ring the correct answers.

● Which of the following words is closest in meaning to **relentlessly**?

incessantly   **happily**   **unkindly**   **cheerfully**

● Where was the Ugly Duckling born?

in a meadow   **on the moor**   **in a field**   **in a farmyard**

● What happened to many of the wild geese he met?

they flew away   **they were killed**   **they teased him**

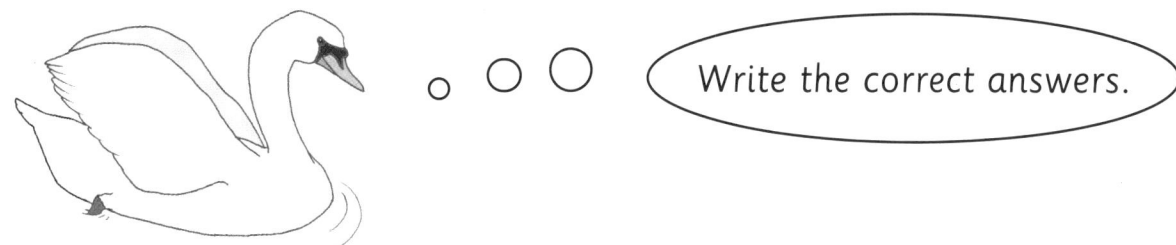

Write the correct answers.

● Write the line of dialogue from the text, that first gives the clue that the Ugly Duckling has developed into an adult swan.

_____

_____

● What made the Ugly Duckling aware that spring was on its way?

_____

_____

● Discuss with a friend, other stories you know in which the central character seems very weak at the beginning but is strong, or the winner, by the end. Write the title of one of them here.

_____

This unit addresses the Literacy Strategy:
Term 2 objective   1: to investigate the styles and voices of traditional story language - collect examples, e.g. story openings and endings; scene
                          openers, e.g. 'Now, when...", "A long time ago...". ; list, compare and use in own writing.
Term 2 objective   2: to identify typical story themes, e.g. trials and forfeits, good over evil, weak over strong, wise over foolish.
Term 2 objective   3: to identify and discuss main and recurring characters, evaluate their behaviour and justify views.

The Hare and the Tortoise
- a fable by Aesop. Part 2.

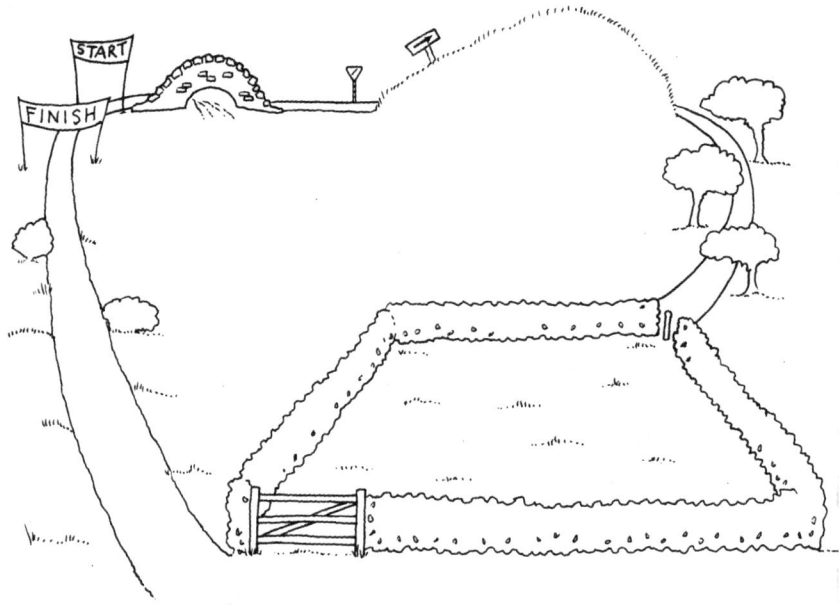

The day of the big race arrived. The animals had prepared a long
course for the race: it started by a bridge, went up the side of a
hill then down the other side. Next there was a long stretch
following a path under the shade of some trees. After the trees,
the route crossed a field, went through a gate, then on to a long
straight lane that led back to the bridge to finish where it started.
At half past ten, the owl called the hare and tortoise forward to
the start. It took two minutes for the tortoise to walk the ten
metres to the starting line!

"Ready, steady, GO!" shouted the owl.

All the animals gasped in amazement as the hare shot over the
bridge and away up the hill. The tortoise hadn't even got
halfway over the bridge by the time the hare was completely out
of sight.

The hare was very pleased with himself.

"This is going to be my easiest race ever," he chuckled to himself.
He slowed down to a walk. By now he was going along the path
through the trees. He felt rather warm so he decided to sit down

The Hare and the Tortoise
- a fable by Aesop. Part 2.

to cool off. He leaned against a tree and closed his eyes.

Back at the bridge, the animals were sitting chatting to each other. "Shouldn't be long," they said. "The hare will be back soon."

Meanwhile the tortoise had slowly made his way up the hill and down the other side. He was plodding along the path through the trees and saw the hare leaning against the tree fast asleep. Slowly and quietly he made his way past the hare. Slowly he trudged across the field, went through the gateway and began to walk along the lane that led to the bridge and the finish line. The horse saw him in the distance.

"Look, there's the tortoise!" he yelled.

"But where's the hare?" said the others. "He's been gone for hours!"

The hare woke up suddenly and stretched himself. He didn't realise that the tortoise had already passed him so he didn't go very fast when he started running again. He crossed the field, went through the gateway, and started running along the lane towards the bridge. "Why are the animals shouting so excitedly?" he wondered to himself. He ran faster and faster but was just in time to see the tortoise cross the finish line.

All the animals rushed to see the tortoise. "Congratulations!" they shouted. "You are the winner."

The hare just sat by the bridge and wondered what had gone wrong.

Read about the route of the race again.

Now put numbers by the phrases below to show their correct order.

We've done one for you.

_____   along the path under some trees

_____   through a gateway

①   over a bridge

_____   across a field

_____   along a straight lane

_____   back to the bridge and the finish line

_____   up the side of a hill and down the other side

**Choose words from the word bank to suit the hare or the
tortoise. Some words can be used for both animals.**

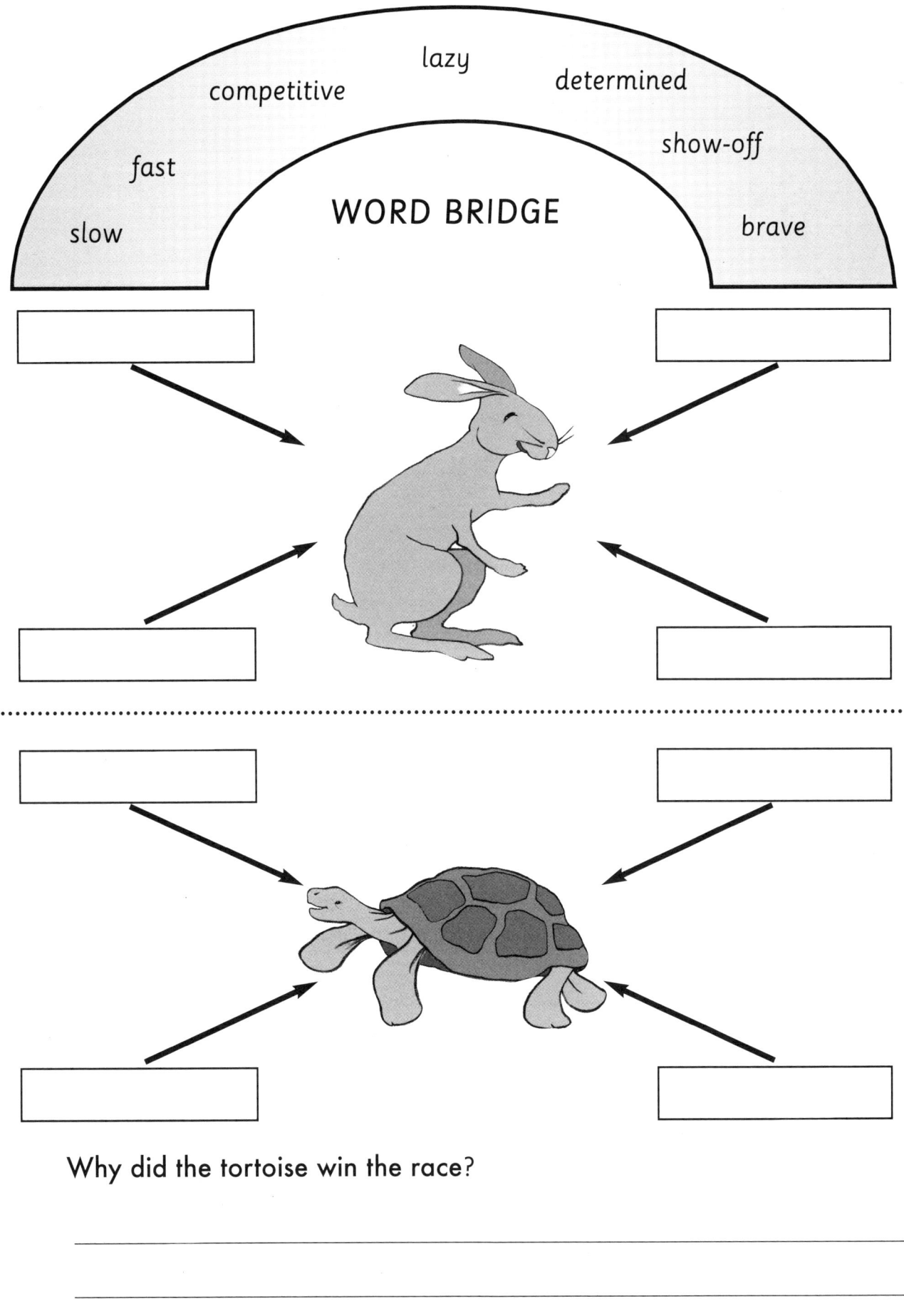

lazy

competitive

determined

fast

show-off

slow

WORD BRIDGE

brave

Why did the tortoise win the race?

_____

_____

This unit addresses the Literacy Strategy:
Term 2 objective   12: to identify the different purposes of instructional texts, e.g. recipes, route-finders, timetables, instructions, plans, rules.
Term 2 objective   14: to how written instructions are organised, e.g. lists, numbered points, diagrams with arrows, bullet points, keys.

YEAR **3** | UNIT **14** | Sheet **A**   Name   Jan's Muffin Cafe

A Recipe for Muffins

Ingredients :   150g self raising flour
                   1/4 teaspoon salt   } sieve
                   1/4 teaspoon baking powder   together

                   40g caster sugar
                   110ml milk
                   50g butter (melted in microwave   } mix
                   or saucepan)   together
                   1 egg

1.   Sieve together the flour, salt and baking powder into a large bowl.

2.   Mix together the sugar, milk, butter and egg in a separate bowl.

3.   Add this to the flour, salt and baking powder and mix with a large spoon quickly for about 20 seconds.

4.   To make your muffins tastier you can now add <u>one</u> of the following:

     50g sultanas   50g chopped apple

     50g raisins   50g blueberries

     50g chopped nuts   50g chocolate drops.

5.   Divide the mixture into 10 cake cases or 6 muffin cases.

6.   Bake in an oven* set at 200°C for 20 to 30 minutes. Remove when lightly brown, using an oven glove, and leave to cool.

     * Make sure an adult is there when you use the oven.

Here is a section from a leaflet about Jan's Coffee and Muffin Cafe.

Visit Jan's Coffee and Muffin Cafe.

This delightful shop can be found in The High Street, Hampton. Twenty different flavours of home-made muffins are served with coffee and other hot and cold drinks.

To find Jan's Coffee and Muffin Cafe -

Coming from the North on the A26, follow the road until you cross over Hazel Road. The cafe will be found on your right.

Coming from the West towards Hampton on the A62. Continue along Hazel Road until you reach the traffic lights. Turn right into the High Street and the cafe will be on your right.

HAMPTON TOWN CENTRE

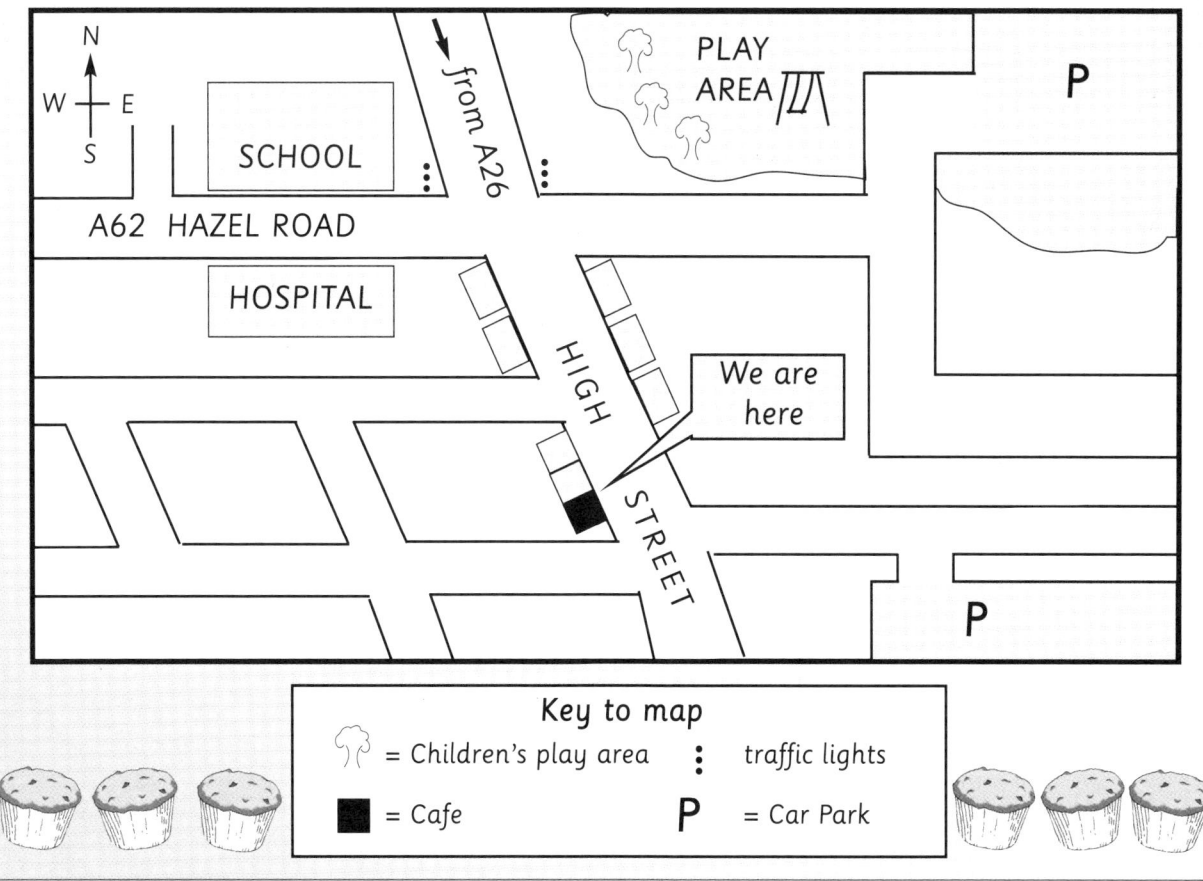

Basic Comprehension

Read the 2 pieces of non-fiction text - the recipe for muffins and the directions to the Coffee and Muffin Cafe.

1.   What is the **first** thing you need to do if you are going to make the muffins? (Tip: you should always do this before you start working on any cooking.)

_____

2.   Which three items should be sieved together?

3.   Why don't we sieve the other items?

_____

_____

4.   Why do you need an adult with you when you use the oven?

_____

_____

5.   Write 3 rules for keeping SAFE in the kitchen. (Think about using the oven, sharp knives and using saucepans safely. Think about keeping tea towels away from the cooker in case they catch fire.)

THREE SAFETY RULES FOR THE KITCHEN.

1._____

_____

2._____

_____

3._____

_____

6.   According to the text, in which street would you find Jan's Coffee and Muffin Cafe? _____

7.   How many different types of muffin would you find in the cafe?   ☐

8.   On the map of Hampton Town Centre how many car parks are there?
     (Look at the key to find the symbol for car park.)   ☐

9.   What building is opposite the school on Hazel Road?

     _____

10.   What symbol is used to mark a children's play area?   ☐

11.   Draw a map, or plan, of the route from the entrance of your
      school to your classroom.
      Write instructions to go with it so that a visitor could find their way to
      your classroom if they had not been to your school.

      ┌───┐
      │   │
      │   │
      │   │
      │   │
      │   │
      │   │
      │   │
      │   │
      │   │
      │   │
      └───┘

      _____

      _____

      _____

      _____

      _____

This unit addresses the Literacy Strategy:
Term 2 objective   12: to identify the different purposes of instructional texts, e.g. recipes, route-finders, timetables, instructions, plans, rules.
Term 2 objective   14: how written instructions are organised, e.g. lists, numbered points, diagrams with arrows, bullet points, keys.

Roam Around Zoo

OPENING TIMES:- MAY – SEPTEMBER ~ EVERY DAY ~ 9.30am – 7.00pm

OCTOBER – APRIL ~ MONDAY – FRIDAY ~ 10.00am – 5.00pm

SATURDAY & SUNDAY ~ 9.30am – 5.30pm

Welcome to Roam Around Zoo. Below you will find a few simple rules which we ask you to abide by, in order to make your visit as pleasant as possible for you, the visitor, and us animals, the residents.

✖ **Do not feed the animals**

- we feed them a balanced diet that keeps them healthy

✔ **Put any litter in the bins provided or take it home with you**

- litter can pose a threat to our livestock
- other visitors will not enjoy a litter strewn park

✖ **Do not make sudden movements or loud noises near the animals**

- a frightened animal can be aggressive

✔ **Open and close aviary doors with care as instructed**

- this will keep our birds in their safe environment

✖ **Do not attempt to climb extra fences placed near large cat enclosures**

- to a lion or tiger you could prove to be a fast snack

✔ **Picnic and Bar-b-que areas are clearly marked, please only use these areas to enjoy your meals**

- litter bins and cooking facilities are provided here

ENJOY YOUR VISIT!

In order to help you enjoy your visit to the full, a timetable of special activities and a map of the zoo can be found on the following page.

Roam Around Zoo

Daily Special Activities

TIME	EVENT	PLACE
10.00 am	Talk about seals, and feeding	Seal Pond
10.30 am	Bird Feeding	Main Aviary
11.00 am	Find out about Kangaroos, Wallabies and Koalas	Australia Enclosure
11.30 am	Feeding time for big cats	Big Cat Arena
Midday	Dolphin Spectacular	Dolphinarium
2.00pm	Parrot Antics	Theatre Square
2.30pm	Talk about seals, and feeding	Seal Pond
3.00pm	Care of pets, talk for children	Pets Corner
4.00pm	Dolphin Spectacular	Dolphinarium
4.30pm	Penguin talk and feeding	Arctic Enclosure

The Roam Around Railway runs every ten minutes. This is free for the use of our visitors, and provides an easy way to get around the park. There are eight stops placed around the zoo.

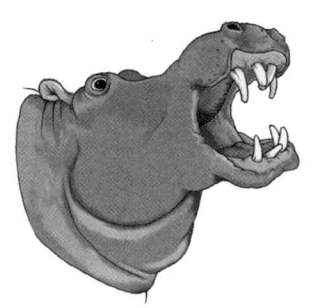

○ ○ ○ Answer these questions
about the zoo.

❖ What is the name of the zoo? _____

❖ How many zoo rules are there? _____

❖ Why should you **not** feed the animals?

_____

_____

❖ What happens at three in the afternoon at Pets Corner?

_____

❖ Where would you go to buy a drink and a cake?

_____

❖ What should you do with your litter?

_____

❖ How many stops are there on the Roam Around Railway?

_____

❖ Which stop would you get off at, if
you wanted to visit the Monkey House? _____

❖ a) What special activity happens at 4.30pm?

_____

b) Where would you go to see this?

_____

❖ **On the back of the sheet.**
Not everyone can read - so make a set of clear picture signs
for the rules. (One sign for each rule.) That way everyone
will know how to behave at Roam Around Zoo.

Name _____   Roam Around Zoo

Now answer these questions about the zoo.

✢ Look at the way the zoo rules have been presented. There is a bullet point for each rule, and extra remarks to indicate the reason for each rule. Why do you think they have been done in this way?

_____

_____

✢ In your own words, (do not use the words in the rules) explain why you should not make a sudden loud noise near the animals.

_____

_____

✢ What creatures might you find in the Reptile House?

_____

✢ What would you find in the places marked **W.C.**? _____

✢ Where would you go to buy a souvenir
of your visit to Roam Around Zoo? _____

✢ How many **different** special
activities take place during the day? _____

✢ A visitor arrived at Roam Around Zoo especially to see the seals being fed. Unfortunately he missed the 10.00am seal feeding - what should he do?

_____

✢ Name three animals you might find in the Australia Enclosure.

_____   _____   _____

✢ **On the back of the sheet, work on your own or with a friend to make a clearly presented set of rules for a swimming pool, a museum or children's playground.**

© Andrew Brodie Publications ✓ www.acblack.com

This unit addresses the Literacy Strategy:
Term 2 objective 14: how written instructions are organised, e.g. lists, numbered points, diagrams with arrows, bullet points, keys.
Term 2 objective 15: to read and follow simple instructions.

YEAR	UNIT	Sheet
3	16	A

Name

Instructions

How To Make a Colour Spinner

You will need:

- ✂ Card
- ✂ Ruler
- ✂ Pair of compasses
- ✂ Scissors
- ✂ Coloured pens or paint
- ✂ A short pencil with a point, or a short pointed stick

What to do:

1. Use your pair of compasses to draw a circle with a diameter of 10cm on to the card - this will be the disc.
2. Cut out the circle.
3. Cut out the template.
4. Divide the disc into seven equal parts using the template to mark the sections.
5. Colour each section so that it matches the diagram.
6. Make a small hole in the middle of the disc and push the pencil or stick through the hole.
7. Spin the disc quickly on a flat surface. What happens?

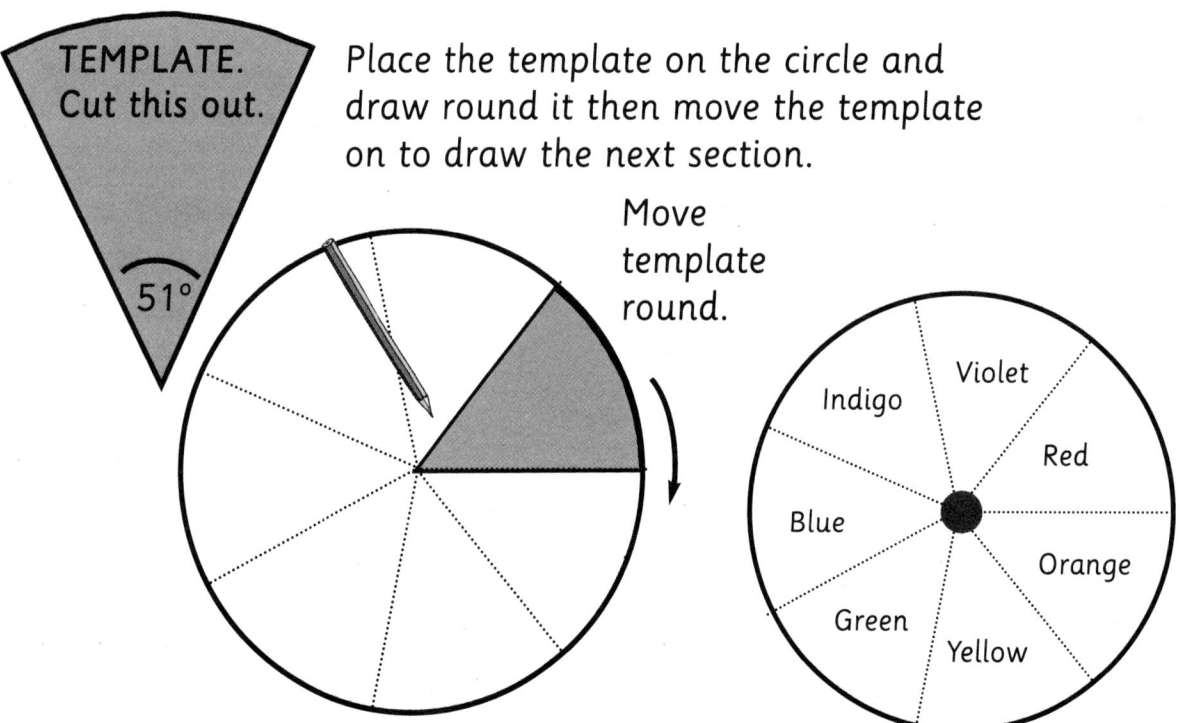

TEMPLATE.
Cut this out.

51°

Place the template on the circle and draw round it then move the template on to draw the next section.

Move template round.

Violet
Indigo
Red
Blue
Orange
Green
Yellow

○ **What is the title of the text? Tick the correct box.**

(Colour Spinners)

(Making Colour Spinners)

(How to make a Colour Spinner)

(How to make a Colour Wheel)

○ **Which section tells you the right order to do things to make the spinner?** _____

_____

○ **Which section tells you what materials you need to make a spinner?**

_____

_____

○ **Why is there a diagram showing all the colours on the spinner?**

_____

_____

○ **What do you do with the pencil or pointed stick?**

_____

_____

○ **Use your dictionary to find out what these colours look like:**

violet _____

_____

indigo _____

_____

○ **Instructions need to be easy to understand and follow. How is the 'What To Do' section organised to make it clear?**

_____

_____

Name _____   Instructions

O Write the first word of each line in the 'What To Do' section.

1. _____ 2. _____ 3. _____

4. _____ 5. _____ 6. _____ 7. _____

O Write four more words of this type.

1. _____ 2. _____ 3. _____ 4. _____

O Why do you think each of these instructions starts with this type of word? _____

_____

O Look at the 'You Will Need' section. How is this organised to make it clear? _____

_____

O Join the correct word to its meaning:

template   a part of something

diagram   a shape to draw round

disc   a drawing that gives information

section   a flat circular shape

O Think of two other times when we might need to write instructions.

1. _____

2. _____

O Read these instructions carefully and do what they ask you to do.
   1. Draw a square which has sides 5cm long.
   2. Draw a line from the top left corner to the bottom right corner.
   3. Put a red dot in the top triangle.
   4. Put a black dot in the bottom triangle.
   5. Draw a black ring round the red dot.
   6. Draw a red ring round the black dot.

Name _____ Instructions

○ Write some instructions for cleaning your teeth. Remember to put a title, bullet points, numbers and diagrams if you need them. Make sure you keep reading what you have written to check that it makes sense and is in the right order. Ask your friends to see if they can follow your instructions.

_____

_____

_____

_____

_____

_____

_____

_____

_____

_____

○ Number these instructions from 1 - 9 in the correct order:

To Make a Cup of Tea

○ When the kettle boils pour the water into the teapot.

○ Pour the tea carefully into the cup.

○ Put a tea bag in the teapot.

○ Put milk in the cups.

○ Drink tea.

○ Put water in the kettle.

○ Wait for the tea to get strong enough.

○ Put in sugar if it is needed and stir.

○ Switch the kettle on to boil.

This unit addresses the Literacy Strategy:
Term 3 objective 1: to retell main points of story in sequence; to compare different stories; to evaluate stories and justify their preferences.
Term 3 objective 2: to refer to significant aspects of the text, e.g. opening, build-up, atmosphere, and to know language is used to create these, e.g. use of adjectives for description.
Term 3 objective 3: to distinguish between 1st and 3rd person accounts.
Term 3 objective 4: to consider credibility of events, e.g. by selecting some real life adventures either written or retold as stories and comparing them with fiction.
Term 3 objective 5: to discuss i) character's feelings, ii) behaviour, e.g. fair or unreasonable, brave or foolish, iii) relationships, referring to the text and making judgements.

My Holiday News - by Andrew

On Friday I flew in an aeroplane from Bristol to Belfast with Mum and Eliza.

We arrived at Bristol Airport two hours before our flight so we had plenty of time to look in the shops.

Mum spent ages looking at the blue glass things that were for sale in one shop. I just had to stand and wait quietly. There was a cool pen made of blue glass. You had to dip it in ink and then you could write with it, but I wasn't allowed to. Eliza was and I don't think that's fair.

When we got on the plane Mum and Eliza looked really worried. I think they're really frightened about flying but I'm not. I held Mum's hand tightly so that she wouldn't be scared.

The flight was great. Sometimes the plane bounced up and down. Mum said it was because of turbulence. That was my favourite bit.

Name   My Holiday News

Read Andrew's holiday news.

Then answer these questions.

1. Where did Andrew's aeroplane leave from?

   _____

   _____

2. Where did Andrew's aeroplane fly to?

   _____

   _____

3. Who was Andrew flying with?

   _____

   _____

4. Describe the item that Andrew liked in the glass shop.

   _____

   _____

5. What did Andrew feel was unfair?

   _____

   _____

6. Why did Andrew hold his Mum's hand?

   _____

   _____

7. What was Andrew's favourite part of the flight?

   _____

   _____

8. Now make up your own question about the passage. You could ask a friend to answer it.

   _____

34 Causeway Road
Belmont
County Antrim
5th September

Dear Gran,

It's very good to be home, although the journey back home was terrible! Andrew had to have a good talking to because he would not behave himself. The trouble started at the airport. I wanted a quick look at the shops. We went into one that sold blue glass items. Andrew found a pen made of glass. He kept dipping it in some ink and writing on a pad of paper. That would be fine but he wouldn't let Eliza have a go. When he did put it down she picked it up, so he snatched it off her and that's when it snapped in two!

On the plane Andrew was terrified. He squeezed my hand tightly and started to cry when we took off. I did feel sorry for him, especially when he screamed when there was turbulence. Thanks for having us to stay.

See you soon.

Love,

Jan

Read Jan's letter...

...then answer these questions.

1. Jan is the mother of which two children?

   _____ and _____

2. Which child was naughty on the journey?

   _____

3a. Describe what Andrew did with the pen, according to Jan's letter?

   _____

   _____

   _____

b. Is this what Andrew described about the pen in his holiday news?

   _____

4a. Describe how Andrew behaved on the plane, according to Jan's letter.

   _____

   _____

   _____

b. Is this how Andrew described the flight? _____

5. Jan and Andrew wrote different descriptions. Who do **you** think is

   right? _____

6. Discuss with a friend whether you think Jan's letter is a good
   'thank you' letter.

This unit addresses the Literacy Strategy:
Term 3 objective   1: to retell main points of story in sequence; to compare different stories; to evaluate stories and justify their preferences.
Term 3 objective   5: to discuss i) character's feelings; ii) behaviour e.g. fair or unreasonable, brave or foolish; iii) relationships, referring to the text and making judgements.

The Story of Serena and Ray
by Dan Dashwood.

Serena was always lonely in the playground. She didn't really have any friends. The others played skipping games together but she wasn't any good at skipping, or ball games for that matter. The other children said she could turn the rope but it wasn't worth having a go at skipping because she was 'out' straight away. So, usually she walked round the edge of the playground or asked to go into the library.

Now, Mrs Silk, like all good teachers, had noticed how lonely Serena was at playtimes. Mrs Silk even talked about friends and 'being left out' in Circle Time but somehow the children didn't seem to notice that Serena was often on her own. It was probably because Serena usually smiled so perhaps they thought she wanted to walk slowly around the playground or sit quietly reading books.

Mrs Silk thought hard about Serena and how she could change things for her, but it was Ray who had the best plan.

Ray had not long been in the class; he was a quiet boy with a round face and big dark eyes. He had a crop of black shiny hair that bounced as he walked along. His school jumper was blue but faded and a bit frayed at the cuffs. It must have been someone else's before because, as I said, he had only come to the school this term.

Ray waited behind one playtime so that he could see Mrs Silk.

"Mrs Silk, at my old school," Ray began, " we had a sort of library loan for playground toys."

"Did you?" said Mrs Silk. "Tell me how it worked."

"Well, we each had a special card and the Friends of the School bought some playground toys for us like bats, balls, dolls, toy cars, ropes, hoops and small games in bags. Then you could swap your card for a toy to play with and at the end of playtime give the toy back and collect your card. If anyone lost their card they could pay 50p for a new one and the money went towards buying new toys. It was run by two children and I thought me and Serena could do it. I never know what to do at playtimes and she doesn't either."

"That sounds like an excellent idea Ray," replied Mrs Silk. "Go and tell Serena your idea and then next playtime you can write a letter to the Friends of the School to see if they would buy some toys."

" We could make the cards on the computer and perhaps some children will have toys at home they don't play with anymore that we could have," Ray replied happily.

Three weeks after Ray stayed behind to speak to Mrs Silk, the playtime toy library had started. Ray and Serena organised it each day, and it was not long before they knew every child in the school.

Basic Comprehension

1. When Serena was in the playground she was:

   ☐ **good at skipping**   ☐ **lonely**

   ☐ **happy**   ☐ **with her friends**

2. Fill in the gaps:

   Ray had a ☐ school jumper which was ☐ at the

   cuffs. His hair was ☐ and his eyes were ☐

   and ☐ .

3. At the start of the story how do you think Serena felt when it was playtime? Put a ring round 3 of the words or group of words which you think best describes how she felt.

happy	**sad**	**lonely**	**cross**	**worried**
annoyed that she couldn't join in	**it was unfair**	**she didn't like the other children**	**the other children didn't like her**	**no one cared how she felt**

4. How did Ray behave? What do we learn about Ray's character in the story? Write 2 sentences about how you feel about him.

   1. Ray was thoughtful because...... —————————————

   _____

   _____

   2. ——————————————————————

   _____

   _____

5. Pretend you are Ray or Serena and write a letter to the Friends of the School to tell them about Ray's idea and ask them if they would buy some playground toys.

This unit addresses the Literacy Strategy:
Term 1 objective   1: to compare a range of story settings, and to select words and phrases that describe scenes.
Term 1 objective   8: to express their views about a story or poem, identifying specific words and phrases to support their viewpoint.
Term 3 objective   5: to discuss i) characters' feelings ii) behaviour, e.g. fair or unreasonable, brave or foolish, iii) relationships, referring to the
                       text and making judgements.

Josh Moves House

Josh was a cheerful nine year old, with dark glossy hair, sparkling brown eyes and a grin that seemed to spread from ear to ear. Today, however, his eyes lacked their usual sparkle and he wore a worried frown. The problem was that Josh and his family were moving.

His parents and his elder brother and sister all seemed very excited at the prospect of a new home. It was bigger than the apartment they were leaving, so the children would be able to have a bedroom each, and there would be a garden to play in. Mum and Dad talked excitedly about having summer barbeques and the older children were planning what colours to decorate their new bedrooms. Josh was the only one who did not relish the imminent move. He knew he should have felt pleased, but he didn't. Josh had always lived in the cosy little apartment, and he simply couldn't believe that anywhere else could ever feel like home.

Moving day arrived. Josh was filled with sadness as he watched the removal men packing everything up. By midday it had all been loaded into the large lorry, and it was time to go to the new house. The family piled into the car, with Josh, as the smallest, in the middle of the back seat.

There were last minute odds and ends packed in the car with them, making Josh feel hot, uncomfortable, and more miserable than ever. He closed his eyes tightly as he couldn't bear to look back at the home he had always felt so happy in. His eyes stung as he fought to hold back the tears that were threatening to flow freely down his cheeks.

After what seemed like an eternity, but in reality was about two hours, the car came to a halt in the driveway of the new house. The removal lorry was already there waiting, and Mum went happily to unlock the doors.

Whilst all the family's belongings were unloaded again, Josh mooched around the new garden feeling very lonely. He felt quite sure he would never belong in this new house.

In the corner of the garden was a small pond. Josh looked down into the water where he spotted three small goldfish. He became absorbed, watching them darting in and out of the weeds. As he sat there, still and quiet, he realised that hiding timidly amongst the marginal plants growing in the shallow water at the edge of the pond were a number of very tiny young fish, which he later learned were called fry. It was simply amazing what a lot there was to see in such a small pond. Josh made a mental note to ask Mum if they could buy some fish food when they next went shopping.

Before he knew it, it was time to go in for tea. He was surprised to see how warm and welcoming the kitchen looked with their old table in it. In fact all their things already looked quite comfortable in their new places. He went to look in his new bedroom feeling rather apprehensive. He was astonished. His toys were there, as was his bed, his desk, his chest of drawers and on the wall were his favourite posters. Suddenly Josh realised this really was home now and he was going to be very happy here.

Basic Comprehension

Ring the correct answer:

1. What is the name of the central character in the story?

    (**Jess**)   (**John**)   (**Josie**)   (**Josh**)

2. How many people are in the family?

    (**three**)   (**four**)   (**five**)   (**six**)

3. How did Josh feel at the beginning of the story?

    (**excited**)   (**cheerful**)   (**mad**)   (**worried**)

4. What type of home were the family leaving?

    (**house**)   (**apartment**)   (**bungalow**)   (**castle**)

5. What type of home were the family moving to?

    (**house**)   (**apartment**)   (**bungalow**)   (**castle**)

Write the answers to the following questions.

6. Which 2 words in the text are used to describe Josh's hair?

    _____   _____

7. How many goldfish did Josh first see darting in and out of the weeds?

    _____

8. Which phrase in the last paragraph tells you that time had passed quickly for Josh while he was watching the fish?

    _____

9. What were on the walls of Josh's new bedroom?

    _____

10. How did Josh feel at the end of the story?

    _____

    _____

Advanced Comprehension

1. In the opening paragraph of the story, which phrases tell you that Josh is not looking forward to moving house?

_____

_____

2. At least how many bedrooms were there in the new house? _____

3. How did you know this?

_____

_____

4. Which sentence in the text tells us that Josh nearly cried in the car?

_____

_____

5. Which of the following phrases means the same as 'imminent'.
   Ring the correct answer?

   (**very nasty**)　　(**very close to happening**)　　(**very distant**)

6. How did Josh's feelings change during the story?

_____

_____

7. Which word in the text tells you that Josh felt
   nervous about looking in his new bedroom? _____

8. Which word tells you that what he sees is a big surprise?

_____

9. On the lines below, write about whether you enjoyed the story.
   Give reasons for your answer.

_____

_____

_____

_____

This unit addresses the Literacy Strategy:
Term 3 objective 6: to compare forms or types of humour, e.g. by exploring, collecting and categorising form or type of humour, e.g. word play, joke poems, word games, absurdities, cautionary tales, nonsense verse, calligrams.
Term 3 objective 7: to select, prepare, read aloud and recite by heart poetry that plays with language or entertains; to recognise rhyme, alliteration and other patterns of sound that create effects.

AMBITION

When I grow up I'll climb
A mountain steep and tall.
Though as I'm very scared of heights
That wouldn't work at all.

When I'm older I might sail
On the ocean or the sea,
But waves can make me seasick
So this isn't the life for me.

Perhaps I'll be a park keeper
And care for the flowers and trees
But, as I suffer hay fever
I'd sneeze and sneeze and sneeze.

I'm very fond of little pests
And all sorts of other creatures.
So I know the perfect job for me;
I think I'll be a teacher!

Words

Are words fun,
Or are they crazy?
Are words energetic
Or just plain lazy?
Why use lots when one will do,
When you say flew or flue or flu?
Is a bill what you pay
Or is it on a bird?
Should bowls be played
Or should they be stirred?
Do I use a bat to strike a ball
Or should it fly at night,
and not be hit at all?

Does a bow shoot an arrow
Or do my hair up tight?
Is a man wearing armour
A night or a knight?
I think I heard a herd of cows
So this is where I'll end
Oh words can be a problem
Or words can be your friend.

WHAT A DAY!

I'm bored!
Well play with your bat and ball.
So I did
But the bat flew away.

I'm bored!
Well go and play on the computer.
So I did
But I was too heavy, the computer broke.

I'm hungry!
Well go and get some chips.
So I did
But they were computer chips.

I'm still bored!
Well go and brush your hair.
So I did
But the hare ran away.

I'm tired!
Well get into bed.
So I did.
I hope mummy will read me a story.

Yummy
Little Jim Horner
Sat in a corner
Eating a bowl of rice.
It was covered in custard,
And very hot mustard.
Jim said, "Goodness me, that was nice!"

A FESTIVE THOUGHT

Christmas is coming
The skies are looking murky.
At this exciting time of year
I'm glad I'm not a turkey!

Mary Had...
Mary had a little lamb
She kept it for the wool.
But when she started knitting,
The lamb said,
"Ouch, don't pull."

ouch!!

Alien Babies
Monday's child is green and red;
Tuesday's child has a very square head;
Wednesday's child is jagged and tall;
Thursday's child is shaped like a ball;
Friday's child looks like a snail;
Saturday's child has a very long tail;
And the child that is born on the seventh night,
Gives all the others a most terrible fright!

Read all the poems before you answer the questions.

❧ Which of the poems did you enjoy most?

_____

❧ Why did you like it best?

_____

_____

❧ In 'Alien Babies' which day of the week is not written in the poem? _____

❧ Write a sentence that contains each of the following words.

flew _____

_____

flue _____

_____

flu _____

_____

❧ Which well known nursery rhyme does 'Yummy' remind you of?

_____

_____

❧ 'What a Day' could be called a **nonsense poem**. Why?

_____

_____

❧ Which of the poems does not use rhyme?

_____

❧ **On the back of the sheet choose one longer poem or two shorter ones to copy in your best handwriting. Illustrate the poem/poems and learn it/them by heart.**

❧ Which three of the poems are based on other well-known rhymes?

_____

_____

_____

❧ Which two of the poems play with word meanings?

_____

_____

❧ In 'Ambition' what are the little pests?

_____

❧ Put each of the following words into a sentence.

knight _____

_____

night _____

_____

heard _____

_____

herd _____

_____

❧ Why would you not want to be a turkey at Christmas?

_____

_____

❧ All the poems were written to make you smile.
  Which one do you think is funniest and why? _____

_____

❧ 'What a Day' does not use rhyme. How do you know it is a poem?

_____

❧ **On the back - try writing either a poem based on a well-known nursery rhyme or a poem that plays with word meanings. Illustrate your final version.**

This unit addresses the Literacy Strategy:
Term 3 objective   16: to read examples of letters written for a range of purposes, e.g. to recount, explain, enquire, complain, congratulate, comment; understand form and layout including use of paragraphs, ways of starting, ending, etc. and ways of addressing different audiences - formal/informal.
Term 3 objective   19: to summarise orally in one sentence the content of a passage or text, and the main point it is making.

YEAR	UNIT	Sheet
3	21	A

Name

Letters

Read this letter out loud to a friend.

35 Stoke Road
Westerton
Yorkshire
YY7 3NT

28th December

Dear Mr and Mrs Williams,

Thank you very much for sending me some money. My mum said that you always gave her presents when she was little because you were Granny's best friend.

I have had really good presents. My best present was a new computer. I am typing this letter on the computer. Thank you again. You are very kind.

Yours sincerely

Kelly

Now read this letter.

35 Stoke Road
Westerton
Yorkshire
YY7 3NT

Computer Supplies
Unit 7
West Industrial Estate
York

25th November

Dear Sir or Madam,

I am enquiring about purchasing a computer and printer suitable for my daughter who is eight years old. I would need to have it delivered by 20th December.

Please send a catalogue and a price list.

Yours faithfully,

Jane Jones.

Mrs. J. Jones

Now read one more letter.

35 Stoke Road

Monday 3rd

Hi Kim,

I'm so excited now it's December. I'm going to buy Mum some perfume. I might get perfume for Granny too.

I want a new computer but I don't think I'll get one because they're so expensive.

Do you think it will snow?

Love from

Kelly

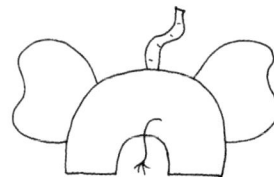

Do you like my elephant?

Basic Comprehension

Answer these questions about the three letters.

1. All three letters were from the same address. Write the address in full.

_____

_____

_____

_____

2. Write the correct description for each letter.

Letter Descriptions

Informal letter to friend.   Formal letter to friend.

Formal business letter.

Letter	Description
To Mr and Mrs Williams	
To Computer Supplies	
To Kim	

Discuss these questions with a friend.

1. What was the main purpose of the letter to Mr and Mrs Williams?

2. What was the main purpose of the letter to Kim?

3. What was the main purpose of the letter to Computer Supplies?

4. Now compare the three letters.
   What differences can you find?

| YEAR 3 | UNIT 22 | Sheet A |

Name

More Letters

Letter 1 ↓

52 Hole Street
Totpen Green
Bartown
Devon
TA21 1GN

Peter Collins
Cool Magazine
20-21 Bent Street
Borford BR21

Dear Mr Collins,

....

Letter 2 ↓

Mum,
I've gone to the cinema with Helen. Will be back about 9pm. See you soon.
Mandy

Letter 3 ↓

12 Sparrow Street
Dunsfield
Kent
MD 17
13 October

Dear Gemma,

....

Letter 4 ↓

Bramble Cottage

Hi John, ...

Letter 5 ↓

from: annsmith@webcom.co.uk
to: sarahsmith@dovetail.co.uk
subject:how are things?
date: 22.4.02   09:14

Dear Sarah, ...

Letter 6 ↓

Holly Cottage
Brown Lane
Laketown
Oxfordshire
OX17 6PT
3 March 2002

Castle Library
Castle Hill
MR 33
Dear Sir/Madam,

....

Look at the six different headings below. They are all headings for different types of letter.

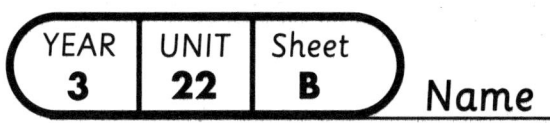

An e-mail message   A short message to a friend

A letter to find out about a job   A letter to a friend

A note   A letter to complain about a magazine

1.   Match the number of the letter with the type of letter you think it is.

Letter 1...

Letter 2...

Letter 3...

Letter 4...

Letter 5...

Letter 6...

2.   Which of the six letters are formal (business-like) and which are informal (friendly)?

FORMAL	INFORMAL

Think of four reasons that we write letters or send messages and notes.

_____

_____

_____

_____

Now read these two letters:

Letter A

Dear Stuart,

    Thanks for your letter. I think it is a really good idea for our class to write to your class in New Zealand. Everybody here was really excited to get the parcel last week, and we couldn't wait to open it.

    By the way, my name is Gary, and I am ten years old. I've got two brothers called Josh and Colin, and one sister, Cynthia, who is a real pain. We live in a small house on the edge of a town.

    I am very glad you like sport, because I do too. Football is my favourite game and I support Man U. Do you play football over there? You said you go to Rugby matches and support The Crusaders - they sound like a cool team. I play with my school team and am usually in goal. I have only let in two goals this year.

    Write soon and tell me more about yourself and New Zealand.

        Your friend,

        Gary

Letter B

Dear Mr Jackson,

    My name is Gary Small, and my class is doing a project about the Second World War. As you were a fighter pilot in the war we were wondering if you would be kind enough to write and tell us what it was like.

    These are some of the things we would like to know. What sort of plane did you fly? Where did you fly to? What did you wear? Were you frightened?

    Any information that you can give us would be really helpful for our project.

    Thank you for taking the time to read this letter and I look forward to hearing from you soon.

        Yours sincerely,

        Gary Small

Look at Letter A

1. Who do you think this letter is to? _____

2. What does the letter tell you about Gary? _____
   _____

3. What do you think is Stuart's favourite sport? _____

4. Which words or phrases tell you that Gary is writing a friendly letter?

   a. _____
   b. _____
   c. _____

5. How does Gary end his letter? _____

Look at Letter B

6. What words or phrases does Gary use to show he is being polite?

   a. _____
   b. _____
   c. _____

10. In which paragraph will you find the following information?

   The reason why he is writing............ Paragraph _____

   The kind of information that he wants...Paragraph _____

   Information about himself............. Paragraph _____

   Thanking the person he is writing to.... Paragraph _____

11. Look at both letters A and B. Discuss with a friend why you think one letter just starts 'Dear Stuart' and the other 'Dear Mr Jackson'.

12. Look at the letter endings below.
    Colour the formal ones red. Colour the informal ones blue.

   (yours sincerely,)   (love from,)   (yours faithfully,)

   (best wishes,)   (lots of love,)   (yours,)

YEAR **3** | UNIT **23** | Sheet **A**   Name   Lots of Letters

Here is an **informal** letter.

Can you tell who received this one?

Miss M. Gardener
Bluebell Cottage
Green Road
LEAFTOWN

FLEDGE COTTAGE
THE DRIFT
HAPPY TOWN

Dear Mary,

Thank you for the lovely day I enjoyed with you last week. I was so pleased to be able to look around your fabulous garden. I would not be surprised if you won the 'best garden' prize in your town this year.

You must have worked exceptionally hard in it to have made it look so colourful. I know some people feel your choice of plants and flowers can be rather contrary, but I was most impressed by the colourful display and originality of the layout of the garden.

The silver bells and cockle shells in the main flower bed looked quite delightful, and the rows of 'pretty maids' bordering the path were very welcoming.

Perhaps next week you would like to have a day at my house, and help me to plan my planting schemes for next year.

Best wishes

Ann

Here are some **formal** letters.

You may know the recipients.

Miss A Hubbard
Cupboard Cottage
FANTASY LAND
BO12 3NE

Mr Cooke
Cake Lane
KITCHEN TOWN

Canine Welfare Agency
1 Doggy Lane
Petsville
2nd August 2003

Dear Miss Hubbard

I am writing to you concerning the welfare of your dog.

It was recently brought to my attention that you had failed to ensure your pet had adequate nourishment. In fact I believe that recently you were unable to provide your pet with a bone to chew.

Within the next week I will contact you to discuss this matter more fully.

Yours sincerely,

Mr Ivor Bone (Canine Welfare Agency)

Munchy House
Pie Lane
Nibbletown
12th Nov 2003

Dear Sir

I am writing to you to investigate the possibility of ordering one of your speciality pies.

Your growing fame as a prizewinning pie maker is most impressive. Last week I read in the newspaper that your latest masterpiece was an amazing pie filled with 24 birds that burst into song when the pie crust was cut. Would you take an order for another of these pies, and if so could you inform me of the cost?

Please reply at your earliest convenience with availability and pricing information.

Yours faithfully

Mr P I Eater.

Ring the correct answer. ◯ ◯ ◦

Which of the following words is nearest in meaning to the word <u>informal</u>?

information   **pleasant**   **interesting**   **unofficial**

Which of the following words is nearest in meaning to the word <u>formal</u>?

unfriendly   **official**   **fortunate**   **complaining**

Which of the following words is nearest in meaning to the word <u>provide</u>?

protect   **please**   **entertain**   **give**

 ◦ ◯ ◯ Write the correct answer.

On the three lines below, write the titles of the nursery rhymes that the letters are connected with?

_____

_____

_____

What is found in the top right-hand corner of each envelope?

_____

What is missing beneath the address on Ann's letter to Mary?

_____

Which of the three letters is a 'thank you' letter?

_____

On the back of the sheet either write a 'nursery rhyme' letter of your own or in your best handwriting write the rhyme that one of the three letters came from.

Name   Lots of Letters

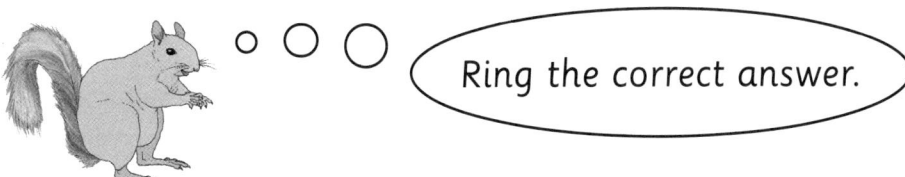

Ring the correct answer.

The person who receives a letter is the

sender   **writer**   **postman**   **recipient**

<u>Adequate</u> means the same as

healthy   **enough**   **plenty**   **starving**

What is the correct way to finish a formal letter that begins 'Dear Sir'?

yours sincerely   **yours faithfully**   **best wishes**   **love from**

Write the answers to the
following questions.

Where does Mr P I Eater live?

_____

_____

Read the first paragraph of each letter. What should the first
paragraph of any letter be about?

_____

_____

In the letter from 'Mr Eater', there is a verb that is spelt
the same in both the past and present tense. Name it.

Which of the letters would you describe as an enquiry?

_____

What goes at the top right-hand corner of a letter?

_____

On the back write a reply to one of the letters. Remember to lay it out
correctly.

This unit addresses the Literacy Strategy:
Term 1 objective   20: to read information passages, and identify main points or gist of text, e.g. by noting or underlining key words or
                               phrases, listing the 4 or 5 key points covered.
Term 3 objective   19: to summarize orally in one sentence the content of a passage or text, and the main point it is making.

YEAR	UNIT	Sheet		The Sun, Moon
3	24	A	Name	and Planets

Read this passage about the Sun carefully and think about what it is telling you. There is a lot of information so you need to decide which parts are the most important.

The Sun

The Sun is a star and gives out light and heat. It is as big as a million Earths, all squashed together. If we imagine the Sun as big as a football, then the Earth would be as small as an apple pip. If you measured the Sun from one side to the other, it would be 109 times the distance across the Earth. Even though the Sun is very big, it is not as big as some of the other stars that we see in the sky. The other stars look smaller than the Sun, because they are much further away. Things that are a long way away always look smaller. If you could stand on the surface of the Sun, you would turn into a crisp very quickly! It is about 6000 degrees Celsius on the surface and much hotter in the centre. An ordinary oven in a kitchen can only reach about 300 degrees Celsius, when it is at its hottest.

Now using only a few sentences, try to tell your partner about what you have just read. Which part of the passage is not true really? Why did the writer put that statement in?

The Moon

Read this passage about the Moon carefully and think about what it is telling you. There is a lot of information so you need to decide which parts are the most important.

The Moon is about 385,000km away from the Earth and is about as wide as Australia. During the day on the Moon it can be hot enough to boil water, but at night it can be freezing. If we look at the moon at night from the Earth, we can see darker and lighter parts. These are the mountains and holes on the Moon. The holes are called craters, and are made when rocks crash into the surface of the moon.

If you were to land on the Moon, you would be able to jump much higher that you can on Earth. You would not be able to breathe, though, as there is no atmosphere on the Moon. You would have to wear a special spacesuit to provide the air you need to live.

Men first landed on the Moon on 20 July 1969. The first man to set foot on the Moon was an American called Neil Armstrong. He had flown there in a space rocket called Apollo 11.

Now using only a few sentences, try to tell your partner about what you have read.

The Planets

There are nine planets that travel around the Sun. Earth is a planet and is just the right distance from the Sun in order that life can survive. If we were any nearer the Sun we would be too hot and if we were further away we would freeze.

Mercury is the name of the planet nearest the Sun. It is very, very hot on Mercury; it is smaller than the Earth. Venus is between Mercury and the Earth and can be seen just using your eyes, if you know where to look.

Jupiter is the biggest planet and you could squeeze all the other planets together inside it. It seems to be made up of gas and liquid that is swirling around – it also has 24 moons!

If you could land on Mars you would see mountains and craters and what look like dried up rivers. If you looked up when you were standing on Mars, the sky would look pink!

Uranus, Neptune and Pluto are so far from the Sun that they are very cold. Pluto is usually the furthest from the Sun but sometimes Neptune is further away. Uranus and Neptune are about four times as big as Earth.

None of the planets have any light of their own. We can only see them because they reflect the Sun's light.

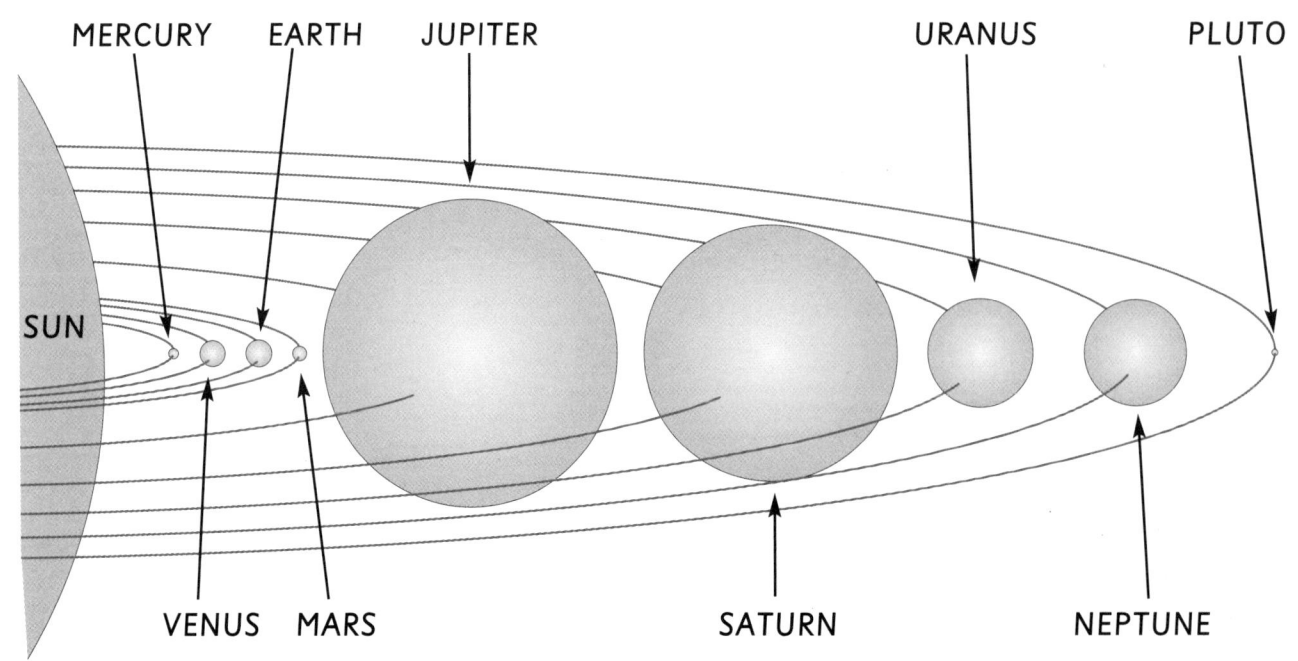

Name _____

The Sun, Moon and Planets

Once you have read the passage about 'The Planets', underline or highlight one fact in the text about each of the planets and then write the fact in the correct place below. One of the planets does not have a special fact mentioned in the text. Use your own research skills to find a fact about this planet. You could try looking in books or on the computer.

Mercury _____

_____

Venus _____

_____

Earth _____

_____

Mars _____

_____

Jupiter _____

_____

Saturn _____

_____

Uranus _____

_____

Neptune _____

_____

Pluto _____

_____

We hope that you have found this book useful. We would be very pleased to receive your comments on this book or to hear your suggestions for new books. If you wish to make any comments or if you would like to be put on our mailing list please contact us:

by telephone: **01480 212666**

by fax: **01480 405014**

by email: **sales@acblack.com**

by post: **A & C Black Publishers**
PO Box 19
St. Neots
Cambs
PE19 8SF

You may wish to photocopy and fax this page to us, completing any of the sections below that you feel relevant:

Name: _____

Address: _____

_____

Telephone: _____

Email address: _____

Comments: _____

_____

_____

_____

_____

_____